Barnes & Noble Shakespeare

David Scott Kastan
Series Editor

BARNES & NOBLE SHAKESPEARE features newly edited texts of the plays prepared by the world's premiere Shakespeare scholars. Each edition provides new scholarship with an introduction, commentary, unusually full and informative notes, an account of the play as it would have been performed in Shakespeare's theaters, and an essay on how to read Shakespeare's language.

DAVID SCOTT KASTAN is the Old Dominion Foundation Professor in the Humanities at Columbia University and one of the world's leading authorities on Shakespeare.

Barnes & Noble Shakespeare
Published by Barnes & Noble
122 Fifth Avenue
New York, NY 10011
www.barnesandnoble.com/shakespeare

Image on p. 286:
William Shakespeare, *Comedies, Histories, & Tragedies*, London, 1623, Bequest of Stephen Whitney Phoenix, Rare Book & Manuscript Library, Columbia University.

Library of Congress Cataloging-in-Publication Data

Shakespeare, William, 1564–1616.
Julius Caesar / William Shakespeare.
  p. cm. — (Barnes and Noble Shakespeare)
Includes bibliographical references.
ISBN-13: 978-1-4114-0040-5
ISBN-10: 1-4114-0040-2
1. Caesar, Julius—Assassination—Drama. 2. Brutus, Marcus Junius, 85?–42 B.C.—Drama. 3. Rome—History—Civil War, 43–31 B.C.—Drama. 4. Conspiracies—Drama. 5. Assassins—Drama. I. Title.

PR2808.A1 2006
822.3'3—dc22

2006018624

Printed and bound in the United States.

23 24 25 26 27 28 29 30

JULIUS CAESAR

William SHAKESPEARE

ANDREW HADFIELD
EDITOR

Barnes & Noble Shakespeare

Contents

Introduction to *Julius Caesar*
by Andrew Hadfield

ulius Caesar is a pivotal play in Shakespeare's career. Performed in 1599, it was probably the first play presented at the newly constructed Globe, a large, expensive theater that Shakespeare's company, the Lord Chamberlain's men, needed to fill. The play itself is tense and dramatic, and, while Shakespeare's audience would have already been familiar with the story, the play offers a fresh and compelling study of the destructive conflict of major historical actors undermined by their own limitations. Topical and allusive, Shakespeare's text dares the audience to make connections between the fall of the Roman Republic and their own times. The play ushered in a new, more mature and confident phase of Shakespeare's writing that saw him produce his major tragedies—*Hamlet*, *Othello*, *King Lear*, and *Macbeth*—in the next few years.

Julius Caesar shows Shakespeare finally realizing the potential that he had always shown throughout his early career. Few Shakespeare plays have been more frequently performed on stage in the last three centuries or studied in schools, demonstrating that what was clearly a successful and popular work in 1599 has captured audiences and readers ever since. Even people who have never seen or read the play can recite "*Et *tu, Brutè?"* and "Friends, Romans, countrymen, lend me your ears." And, like many of the most celebrated literary works, *Julius Caesar* inspires controversy and occasionally conspiracy theories, with some readers even regarding the play as a religious allegory (Julius Caesar, after all, has the same initials as Jesus Christ) and the assassination of Caesar as a mythical event of cosmic significance.

The question that has dominated critical interpretation has been which political faction Shakespeare represents with greater sympathy. Does he tilt toward the republicans, representing Brutus as the "noblest Roman of them all," as Antony declares him to be at the end of the play? Or does he recoil in horror at the dreadful act of violence at the heart of the play, showing us that the republican faction is a group of deluded revolutionaries who have murdered a great hero whose flaws are insubstantial? Perhaps the dominant mode of reading *Julius Caesar* has been to assume that Shakespeare is wisely commenting on the follies of human history, revealing to us that violence inevitably fails to reform corrupt government, only exaggerating the miseries of the suffering people who have had to live under a repressive regime.

There is much to recommend this reading, even if it conveniently reproduces the familiar idea that Shakespeare was a conservative figure who had an instinctive hatred of crowds and mob rule, frequently warning his audience and readers against the follies of premature, rash action. The play does suggest that Caesar is probably not the dreadful tyrant who has sometimes been portrayed, especially in productions that have sought to represent him as a fascist dictator. Caesar is feeble and ailing, deaf in one ear and lacking a robust physical presence, not a vigorous and driven ideologue. Dreadful crimes are committed in his name, such as the silencing of the tribunes, Murellus and Flavius, who object to the celebrations for his victories over Pompey, but they are not necessarily authorized by him. He is arrogant and naïve, especially when he refuses to listen to good advice, and he has little idea of how to govern those who surround him or, indeed what they are planning and how they might feel about him.

But, as Brutus admits in his orchard (2.1.10–34), Caesar has to be killed not because of what he has done but because of what he might do, logic that is problematic on a number of levels, not least because Caesar is hardly unformed. Nevertheless, even if he is no towering twentieth-century dictator, as he has often been represented in more recent productions of the play, Caesar is hardly a straightforwardly admirable character. The opening scene is a reminder that Caesar has achieved power through his triumph over his rival, Pompey, and that he has been prepared to fight a bloody and divisive civil war to rule in Rome. His ally, Mark Antony, delivers a superb funeral oration for his dead friend and leader, but is prepared to rip the social fabric of Rome apart for his own personal revenge.

The republican faction is itself undeniably flawed, and only the most partisan reader could argue that Shakespeare nails his colors to their mast. Cassius is sly and underhanded, having enough knowledge of human behavior to flatter Brutus into joining his cause by throwing stones at Brutus's window and claiming that the people are demanding that Brutus act to save them. Even if Cassius's devoted, homoerotic regard for Brutus humanizes him in the last two acts as the republican forces are hunted down and destroyed, it is still hard not to feel that Cassius, like Mark Antony, allows personal loyalties to override any sense of allegiance to wider communities or feelings of responsibility toward other human beings whose fates he is able to control.

Brutus is undoubtedly a man of principle and constancy, yet he often behaves ridiculously. His speech justifying the assassination of Caesar is based on shaky premises and faulty logic. He delivers another flat speech (3.2.12–46) when needing to persuade the people to support the actions of the conspirators, failing to make a series of specific points against Caesar (that his military background renders him incapable of appreciating the complex nature of Roman government, that he was prepared to wage a brutal civil war to get what he wanted) and concentrating instead on Caesar's abstract and hardly capital crime of "ambition." He is aloof and cold as both friend and husband, refusing to discuss matters with his intelligent and faithful wife who is prepared to wound and finally kill herself because of him, and then failing to see how crucial his alliance with Cassius is as their campaign becomes more and more desperate. Most important, his judgment is often simply wrong, and he is too arrogant to realize how foolish his actions are. He allows Antony to speak at Caesar's funeral against the sage advice of Cassius, who realizes Antony's ability to undermine their cause. He insists that they all bathe in Caesar's blood after they have killed Caesar as a sign of their commitment to "Peace, freedom, and liberty," a moment of grim comedy. And he insists on immediately engaging the army of the triumvirate when no prudent general would take such an absurd risk.

Brutus, as these character summaries indicate, is easily the most important figure in the play (Caesar, after all, dies in Act Three), and *Julius Caesar* has sometimes been read as his tragedy. However, we may wish to resist such efforts to see the play as the tragedy of a single heroic individual. Greek tragedy, and Aristotle's influential reading of the body of drama that defined European theater, emphasized that the action could carry the tragic effect rather than the audience needing to see one figure as a tragic hero. Shakespeare's play can be read as a comment on the tragic state of Rome as the city was in the painful process of transforming itself from a republic to an empire. The characters and their personalities matter less than the situations that they find themselves in and the limited solutions at their disposal.

Roman history was taught in all Elizabethan schools, and everyone who had had an education—and many who had not—knew the basic history of the ancient city-state, knowledge that cannot be taken for granted today. Roman history was widely believed to be cyclical in nature. Rome was traditionally thought to have been founded by its first king, Romulus, who killed his brother Remus after a quarrel. A series of dynasties ruled Rome until the Tarquins, the last kings of Rome, assumed control. Their rule ended when Tarquinus Sextus, the son of the tyrannical king Tarquinus Superbus, raped the chaste Roman matron Lucrece, as Shakespeare narrated in his own version of the story, *The Rape of Lucrece* (1594). Unable to live with her shame, Lucrece killed herself, and the angry Romans, led by Brutus's ancestor, Lucius Junius Brutus, rose up and exiled the Tarquins, vowing never to be ruled by kings again. In place of the monarchy, they established the Roman Republic, a stable form of state that treated all citizens relatively equally, trusting the senators who met in the Capitol building to determine how the city should be governed in consultation with other officials such as the tribunes (elected by the plebeians to represent them).

The Republic was a remarkably successful institution, working through a series of checks and balances to chart a middle course against extremes. Nonetheless, it came under severe pressure as Rome expanded into an empire, in part because it now had to govern vast areas that were hard to control and in part because the army became an increasingly powerful element of Roman society that sought more control for itself. The Republic began to degenerate as feuding factions of generals, inflated by their own triumphs, threatened the fabric of government. Pompey the Great clashed with Julius Caesar, the latter triumphing and becoming dictator. Although Caesar was then assassinated, a series of bloody civil wars erupted throughout the empire until Octavius stood alone as sole ruler of Rome, crowning himself as its first emperor, Augustus. His reign was controversial, having been supported and condemned in equal measure by subsequent historians. But he was followed by some of the most brutal dictators in world history: the infamous Tiberius, Caligula, and Nero. During their reigns, many of the works that the Elizabethans studied were written, including the influential histories by Tacitus and Livy as well as the republican anti-epic by Lucan, the *Pharsalia*.

It is little wonder that the legacy of the Republic was regarded with much more enthusiasm than that of the vicious early days of the Empire.

As this brief overview suggests, Roman history seemed straightforward and easy to remember, and readers were encouraged to make comparisons with events in their own times. Early audiences of *Julius Caesar* were clearly in a position to make such connections when they saw the play, given the ubiquity of Roman history and the wealth of comparisons made between the history of Rome and the history of England by Shakespeare's contemporaries (see "*Julius Caesar* on the Early Stage," page 291). The Rome we see represented on stage in Shakespeare's play is a frightened, paranoid, and vicious place in which individuals find that they can trust no one outside a select circle of close friends because there are no public institutions left to support debate and proper government. The city Shakespeare depicts bears little comparison to that of the Republic at its most stable, when Rome was famed for public oratory and political debate. While the Republic staged great trials of miscreants in which famed orators argued the merits of cases and political decisions were openly debated by all citizens, in *Julius Caesar* individuals hide in corners planning violent acts of desperation. A more pointed contrast still is that between Brutus the founder of the Roman Republic and Brutus the assassin. While the actions of the first Brutus do actually lead to "Peace, freedom, and liberty," those of the second, despite the rallying cry, lead only to chaos and civil war, the death of the incumbent ruler only leading to more deaths.

We must not, however, blame this failure to live up to the ideals of the Republic simply on the characters in Shakespeare's play. A companion piece to *Julius Caesar* is *Hamlet*, another drama centered on a political assassination in which the frustrated and doomed hero exclaims, "The time is out of joint. O cursèd spite, / That ever I was born to set it right" (1.5.188–189). Hamlet realizes the weight of the unwelcome burden that has been thrust upon him and which he would never have chosen himself. The same dilemma confronts the characters in *Julius Caesar*, especially Brutus. That he fails to reproduce the results of his predecessor and namesake suggests that when history does repeat itself it is invariably a pale shadow or a parody of what went before. The time was ripe for the transformation of Rome when the Tarquins ruled. They were genuine tyrants who needed to be overthrown, and there was a popular will that meant that the Republic became a realizable possibility. Julius Caesar is only a potential tyrant, not obviously worse than those men who surround him, and the popular will for the revitalization of the Republic is faked by Cassius. Far from exhibiting a union of leaders and populace, the play shows the conspirators huddling in small groups nervously making grand plans while the people celebrate the achievements of Caesar and ignore the attempts of the tribunes to stir up sympathy for the Republic. As in *Hamlet*, the time is out of joint, and things cannot be put right.

The Republic was able to function so well in the first place because of two central features. One of these was the esteem in which Romans regarded eloquence in speech and writing, including eloquence in political speech, forensic oratory, forms of praise, treatises, letters, works of fiction, and dialogues. The second was the value Romans placed upon friendship, which bound citizens together in a common enterprise. We see eloquence go badly awry in *Julius Caesar*. Caesar himself makes no important speech and concentrates instead on oracular pronouncements that are invariably bizarre and reveal more about his own sense of his self-worth than about anything in the world beyond his ego, a worrying but all too familiar tendency of the isolated dictator. He frequently refers to himself in the third person, as though he had already become a god (an obsession of later Roman emperors). When Calphurnia does manage to persuade him—albeit briefly—that he ought not attend the Senate on the Ides of March, he informs Decius, who has come to collect him, that he will not falsely claim to be sick:

> Shall Caesar send a lie?
> Have I in conquest stretched mine arm so far
> To be afeard to tell graybeards the truth?
> Decius, go tell them Caesar will not come. (2.2.65–68)

Decius asks for a cause to be given so that he can avoid humiliation but is told that the cause is simply Caesar's will. And yet, as we all know, Caesar is eventually persuaded to attend when a more flattering interpretation is given of his wife's frightening dream.

Such words hardly resemble the achievements of the Roman Republic in its heyday, represented for Elizabethans mainly by the works of Cicero, the eloquent and outspoken conscience of the Republic. Cicero produced a whole library of important works, including dialogues, orations made in the Senate and in famous trials, and treatises, most famously on the duties of a citizen, the value of friendship, and the elements of the republican constitution. Cicero was a master of the art of rhetoric, able to tailor any argument to an appropriate form in order to persuade an audience of his position, whether praising great men, prosecuting wrongdoers, or reminding citizens of their loyalty to their country. Cicero does indeed appear in Shakespeare's play, but only as a minor figure. Cicero appears in the third scene of the play, during the great storm that marks the onset of the action once the conspirators have made their decision to kill Caesar. Like Caesar—but for different reasons—he says little, in contrast to the known record of his loquaciousness and ability to manipulate words better than anyone else. Cicero refuses to join the conspirators and appears a calm presence in contrast to the intensely nervous Casca. We eventually learn that he has been put to death. Nonetheless, Cicero's reputation and his role in promoting the virtues of republican Rome cast a shadow over the action of the play. The fact that he has little chance to speak or act in *Julius Caesar* is a potent sign that his values cannot flourish in the cloak-and-dagger world of the play; the eloquent speech and writing that Rome at its best produced and promoted are now irrelevant. Cicero may disparage the aims of the conspirators as well as the actions of Caesar, and stand above the superstition and chaos that envelop Rome, but he is powerless to change the course of the city's destiny.

It is a sad fact that republicans such as Brutus are poor orators—partly because they have no investment in or experience of trying to persuade an audience of citizens that they are right—whereas their most significant opponent, Mark Antony, is a brilliant orator, attentive to the needs and demands of the situation, fully in command of his material, and sensitive to what his audience wants to hear. There is, of course, considerable irony in the fact that Antony is able to derail the republican cause using its own traditional virtues. Not only does he demonstrate that he is a more eloquent speaker than any of his opponents, but he also does what he does for the sake of his dead friend, Julius Caesar. The tables are neatly turned, a further sign of the times when nothing stays in one place. The irony multiplies when, in *Antony and Cleopatra* (1606), Antony meets a similar fate as he dies fighting his erstwhile allies while the Roman Republic implodes from within.

Antony's touching but dangerous loyalty to Caesar is balanced by the friendship between Cassius and Brutus. We witness a world in which the virtues of friendship should lead to stronger ties that enhance and bond the social fabric of the state, but, in fact, here they help to undermine it. Cassius's highly charged love for Brutus helps to persuade him to hatch the plot to assassinate Caesar, a telling example of virtue turned to vice, while Brutus's love for Cassius leads him consistently into terrible errors of judgment. At the end of the play Antony praises Brutus as the "noblest Roman of them all," excusing him from acting against Caesar out of impure motives, unlike his allies, who he argues acted out of "envy of great Caesar" (5.5.69). Antony has missed what is obvious to the audience: just as he acted out of love for Caesar—and was prepared to countenance virtually any consequence to avenge his dead friend—so did Cassius act out of his devotion to Brutus as well as his hatred of Caesar. The two friendships serve to destroy the Republic, the very state that encouraged men to develop such relationships with each other, another keen irony that shadows the play.

The most eagerly anticipated scene in the play for much of its stage history was the quarrel between Brutus and Cassius in Act Four, scene three. Here we see the two doomed generals talking at cross purposes and revealing a breach that can never be healed, one that fatally undermines their military strategy. Cassius and Brutus have vastly different values. Cassius values his friendship with Brutus before all else, so much so that he wants Brutus's regard for him to obscure any sense of Cassius's human flaws. Brutus, in contrast, wants Cassius to adhere to an absolute scale of moral values that no one but the "noblest Roman of them all" could possibly achieve. Their division is not only a pitiful human tragedy, one of the many contained in this remarkable play, but an indication of the collapse of generally accepted values that characterizes the fall of the Roman Republic.

Julius Caesar is a splendid play: complicated, controversial, full of intense dramatic moments, and eloquent even when lack of eloquence is represented on stage. Shakespeare clearly wanted his audience to make connections between the events that finally destroyed the Roman Republic and the impending death of Tudor England. Was England descending into chaos with the absence of a proper central authority, as Elizabeth grew ever older and, according to many of her subjects, remote from the needs and desires of the people she governed? Were her chief courtiers acting like the Roman senators who eventually decided to assassinate their leader, even if they would never dare to commit such a sacrilegious act? Would her death plunge the land into a civil war like the one that had torn Rome apart? Of course, this is not to insist that all readers and audiences bear such connections in mind each time they experience the play. _Julius Caesar_ is a tragedy that cannot be limited to the interests and anxieties that surrounded its first production. As Shakespeare's best-known Roman play, it has inspired a range of creative interpretations, and the dangers of unchecked tyranny, like those of self-deceived would-be saviors, are known in every age. Nevertheless, understanding the Roman history that Shakespeare imaginatively recreates enables us to appreciate the significance, range, and depth of the meanings of the play.

Shakespeare and His England
by David Scott Kastan

hakespeare is a household name, one of those few that don't need a first name to be instantly recognized. His first name was, of course, William, and he (and it, in its Latin form, *Gulielmus*) first came to public notice on April 26, 1564, when his baptism was recorded in the parish church of Stratford-upon-Avon, a small market town about ninety miles northwest of London. It isn't known exactly when he was born, although traditionally his birthday is taken to be April 23rd. It is a convenient date (perhaps too convenient) because that was the date of his death in 1616, as well as the date of St. George's Day, the annual feast day of England's patron saint. It is possible Shakespeare was born on the 23rd; no doubt he was born within a day or two of that date. In a time of high rates of infant mortality, parents would not wait long after a baby's birth for the baptism. Twenty percent of all children would die before their first birthday.

Life in 1564, not just for infants, was conspicuously vulnerable. If one lived to age fifteen, one was likely to live into one's fifties, but probably no more than 60 percent of those born lived past their mid-teens. Whole towns could be ravaged by epidemic disease. In 1563, the year before Shakespeare was born, an outbreak of plague claimed over one third of the population of London. Fire, too, was a constant threat; the thatched roofs of many houses were highly flammable, as well as offering handy nesting places for insects and rats. Serious crop failures in several years of the decade of the 1560s created food shortages, severe enough in many cases to lead to the starvation of the elderly and the infirm, and lowering the resistances of many others so that between 1536 and 1560 influenza claimed over 200,000 lives.

Shakespeare's own family in many ways reflected these unsettling realities. He was one of eight children, two of whom did not survive their first year, one of whom died at age eight; one lived to twenty-seven, while the four surviving siblings died at ages ranging from Edmund's thirty-nine to William's own fifty-two years. William married at an unusually early age. He was only eighteen, though his wife was twenty-six, almost exactly the norm of the day for women, though men normally married also in their mid- to late twenties. Shakespeare's wife Anne was already pregnant at the time that the marriage was formally confirmed, and a daughter, Susanna, was born six months later, in May 1583. Two years later, she gave birth to twins, Hamnet and Judith. Hamnet would die in his eleventh year.

If life was always at risk from what Shakespeare would later call "the thousand natural shocks / That flesh is heir to" (*Hamlet*, 3.1.61–62), the incessant threats to peace were no less unnerving, if usually less immediately life threatening. There were almost daily rumors of foreign invasion and civil war as the Protestant Queen Elizabeth assumed the crown in 1558 upon the death of her Catholic half sister, Mary. Mary's reign had been marked by the public burnings of Protestant "heretics," by the seeming subordination of England to Spain, and by a commitment to a ruinous war with France, that, among its other effects, fueled inflation and encouraged a debasing of the currency. If, for many, Elizabeth represented the hopes for a peaceful and prosperous Protestant future, it seemed unlikely in the early days of her rule that the young monarch could hold her England together against the twin menace of the powerful Catholic monarchies of Europe and the significant part of her own population who were reluctant to give up their old faith. No wonder the Queen's principal secretary saw England in the early years of Elizabeth's rule as a land surrounded by "perils many, great and imminent."

In Stratford-upon-Avon, it might often have been easy to forget what threatened from without. The simple rural life, shared by about 90 percent of the English populace, had its reassuring natural rhythms and delights. Life was structured by the daily rising and setting of the sun, and by the change of seasons. Crops were planted and harvested; livestock was bred, its young delivered; sheep were sheared, some livestock slaughtered. Market days and fairs saw the produce and crafts of the town arrayed as people came to sell and shop—and be entertained by musicians, dancers, and troupes of actors. But even in Stratford, the lurking tensions and dangers could be daily sensed. A few months before Shakespeare was born, there had been a shocking "defacing" of images in the church, as workmen, not content merely to whitewash over the religious paintings decorating the interior as they were ordered, gouged large holes in those felt to be too "Catholic"; a few months after Shakespeare's birth, the register of the same church records another deadly outbreak of plague. The sleepy market town on the northern bank of the gently flowing river Avon was not immune from the menace of the world that surrounded it.

This was the world into which Shakespeare was born. England at his birth was still poor and backward, a fringe nation on the periphery of Europe. English itself was a minor language, hardly spoken outside of the country's borders. Religious tension was inescapable, as the old Catholic faith was trying determinedly to hold on, even as Protestantism was once again anxiously trying to establish itself as the national religion. The country knew itself vulnerable to serious threats both from without and from within. In 1562, the young Queen, upon whom so many people's hopes rested, almost fell victim to smallpox, and in 1569 a revolt of the Northern earls tried to remove her from power and restore Catholicism as the national religion. The following year, Pope Pius V pronounced the excommunication of "Elizabeth, the pretended queen of England" and forbade Catholic subjects obedience to the monarch on pain of their own excommunication. "Now we are in an evil way and going to the devil," wrote one clergyman, "and have all nations in our necks."

It was a world of dearth, danger, and domestic unrest. Yet it would soon dramatically change, and Shakespeare's literary contribution would, for future generations, come to be seen as a significant measure of England's remarkable transformation. In the course of Shakespeare's life, England, hitherto an unsophisticated and under-developed backwater acting as a bit player in the momentous political dramas taking place on the European continent, became a confident, prosperous, global presence. But this new world was only accidentally, as it is often known today, "The Age of Shakespeare." To the degree that historical change rests in the hands of any individual, credit must be given to the Queen. This new world arguably was "The Age of Elizabeth," even if it was not the Elizabethan Golden Age, as it has often been portrayed.

The young Queen quickly imposed her personality upon the nation. She had talented councilors around her, all with strong ties to her of friendship or blood, but the direction of government was her own. She was strong willed and cautious, certain of her right to rule and convinced that stability was her greatest responsibility. The result may very well have been, as historians have often charged, that important issues facing England were never dealt with head-on and left to her successors to settle, but it meant also that she was able to keep her England unified and for the most part at peace.

Religion posed her greatest challenge, though it is important to keep in mind that in this period, as an official at Elizabeth's court said, "Religion and the commonwealth cannot be parted asunder." Faith then was not the largely voluntary commitment it is today, nor was there any idea of some separation of church and state. Religion was literally a matter of life and death, of salvation and damnation, and the Church was the Church of England. Obedience to it was not only a matter of conscience but also of law. It was the single issue on which the nation was most likely to be torn apart.

Elizabeth's great achievement was that she was successful in ensuring that the Church of England became formally a Protestant Church, but she did so without either driving most of her Catholic subjects to sedition or alienating the more radical Protestant community. The so-called "Elizabethan Settlement" forged a broad Christian community of what has been called prayer-book Protestantism, even as many of its practitioners retained, as a clergyman said, "still a smack and savor of popish principles." If there were forces on both sides who were uncomfortable with the Settlement—committed Protestants, who wanted to do away with all vestiges of the old faith, and convinced Catholics, who continued to swear their allegiance to Rome—the majority of the country, as she hoped, found ways to live comfortably both within the law and within their faith. In 1571, she wrote to the Duke of Anjou that the forms of worship she recommended would "not properly compel any man to alter his opinion in the great matters now in controversy in the Church." The official toleration of religious ambiguity, as well as the familiar experience of an official change of state religion accompanying the crowning of a new monarch, produced a world where the familiar labels of Protestant and Catholic failed to define the forms of faith that most English people practiced. But for Elizabeth, most matters of faith could be left to individuals, as long as the Church itself, and Elizabeth's position at its head, would remain unchallenged.

In international affairs, she was no less successful with her pragmatism and willingness to pursue limited goals. A complex mix of prudential concerns about religion, the economy, and national security drove her foreign policy. She did not have imperial ambitions; in the main, she wanted only to be sure there would be no invasion of England and to encourage English trade. In the event, both goals brought England into conflict with Spain, determining the increasingly anti-Catholic tendencies of English foreign policy and, almost accidentally, England's emergence as a world power. When Elizabeth came to the throne, England was in many ways a mere satellite nation to the Netherlands, which was part of the Hapsburg Empire that the Catholic Philip II (who had briefly and unhappily been married to her predecessor and half sister, Queen Mary) ruled from Spain; by the end of her reign England was Spain's most bitter rival.

The transformation of Spain from ally to enemy came in a series of small steps (or missteps), no one of which was intended to produce what in the end came to pass. A series of posturings and provocations on both sides led to the rupture. In 1568, things moved to their breaking point, as the English confiscated a large shipment of gold that the Spanish were sending to their troops in the Netherlands. The following year saw the revolt of the Catholic earls in Northern England, followed by the papal excommunication of the Queen in 1570, both of which were by many in England assumed to be at the initiative, or at very least with the tacit support, of Philip. In fact he was not involved, but England under Elizabeth would never again think of Spain as a loyal friend or reliable ally. Indeed, Spain quickly became its mortal enemy. Protestant Dutch rebels had been opposing the Spanish domination of the Netherlands since the early 1560s, but, other than periodic financial support, Elizabeth had done little to encourage them. But in 1585, she sent troops under the command of the Earl of Leicester to support the Dutch rebels against the Spanish. Philip decided then to launch a full-scale attack on England, with the aim of deposing Elizabeth and restoring the Catholic faith. An English assault on Cadiz in 1587 destroyed a number of Spanish ships, postponing Philip's plans, but in the summer of 1588 the mightiest navy in the world, Philip's grand armada, with 132 ships and 30,493 sailors and troops, sailed for England.

By all rights, it should have been a successful invasion, but a combination of questionable Spanish tactics and a fortunate shift of wind resulted in one of England's greatest victories. The English had twice failed to intercept the armada off the coast of Portugal, and the Spanish fleet made its way to England, almost catching the English ships resupplying in Plymouth. The English navy was on its heels, when conveniently the Spanish admiral decided to anchor in the English Channel off the French port of Calais to wait for additional troops coming from the Netherlands. The English attacked with fireships, sinking four Spanish galleons, and strong winds from the south prevented an effective counterattack from the Spanish. The Spanish fleet was pushed into the North Sea, where it regrouped and decided its safest course was to attempt the difficult voyage home around Scotland and Ireland, losing almost half its ships on the way. For many in England the improbable victory was a miracle, evidence of God's favor for Elizabeth and the Protestant nation. Though war with Spain would not end for another fifteen years, the victory over the armada turned England almost overnight into a major world power, buoyed by confidence that they were chosen by God and, more tangibly, by a navy that could compete for control of the seas.

From a backward and insignificant Hapsburg satellite, Elizabeth's England had become, almost by accident, the leader of Protestant Europe. But if the victory over the armada signaled England's new place in the world, it hardly marked the end of England's travails. The economy, which initially was fueled by the military buildup, in the early 1590s fell victim to inflation, heavy taxation to support the war with Spain, the inevitable wartime disruptions of trade, as well as crop failures and a general economic downturn in Europe. Ireland, over which England had been attempting to impose its rule since 1168, continued to be a source of trouble and great expense (in some years costing the crown nearly one fifth of its total revenues). Even when the most organized of the rebellions, begun in 1594 and led by Hugh O'Neill, Earl of Tyrone, formally ended in 1603, peace and stability had not been achieved.

But perhaps the greatest instability came from the uncertainty over the succession, an uncertainty that marked Elizabeth's reign from its beginning. Her near death from smallpox in 1562 reminded the nation that an unmarried queen could not insure the succession, and Elizabeth was under constant pressure to marry and produce an heir. She was always aware of and deeply resented the pressure, announcing as early as 1559: "this shall be for me sufficient that a marble stone shall declare that a queen, having reigned such a time, lived and died a virgin." If, however, it was for her "sufficient," it was not so for her advisors and for much of the nation, who hoped she would wed. Arguably Elizabeth was the wiser, knowing that her unmarried hand was a political advantage, allowing her to diffuse threats or create alliances with the seeming possibility of a match. But as with so much in her reign, the strategy bought temporary stability at the price of longer-term solutions.

By the mid 1590s, it was clear that she would die unmarried and without an heir, and various candidates were positioning themselves to succeed her. Enough anxiety was produced that all published debate about the succession was forbidden by law. There was no direct descendant of the English crown to claim rule, and all the claimants had to reach well back into their family history to find some legitimacy. The best genealogical claim belonged to King James VI of Scotland. His mother, Mary, Queen of Scots, was the granddaughter of James IV of Scotland and Margaret Tudor, sister to Elizabeth's father, Henry VIII. Though James had right on his side, he was, it must be remembered, a foreigner. Scotland shared the island with England but was a separate nation. Great Britain, the union of England and Scotland, would not exist formally until 1707, but with Elizabeth's death early in the morning of March 24, 1603, surprisingly uneventfully the thirty-seven-year-old James succeeded to the English throne. Two nations, one king: King James VI of Scotland, King James I of England.

Most of his English subjects initially greeted the announcement of their new monarch with delight, relieved that the crown had successfully been transferred without any major disruption and reassured that the new King was married with two living sons. However, quickly many became disenchanted with a foreign King who spoke English with a heavy accent, and dismayed even further by the influx of Scots in positions of power. Nonetheless, the new King's greatest political liability may well have been less a matter of nationality than of temperament: he had none of Elizabeth's skill and ease in publicly wooing her subjects. The Venetian ambassador wrote back to the doge that the new King was unwilling to "caress the people, nor make them that good cheer the late Queen did, whereby she won their loves."

He was aloof and largely uninterested in the daily activities of governing, but he was interested in political theory and strongly committed to the cause of peace. Although a steadfast Protestant, he lacked the reflexive anti-Catholicism of many of his subjects. In England, he achieved a broadly consensual community of Protestants. The so-called King James Bible, the famous translation published first in 1611, was the result of a widespread desire to have an English Bible that spoke to all the nation, transcending the religious divisions that had placed three different translations in the hands of his subjects. Internationally, he styled himself *Rex Pacificus* (the peace-loving king). In 1604, the Treaty of London brought Elizabeth's war with Spain formally to an end, and over the next decade he worked to bring about political marriages that might cement stable alliances. In 1613, he married his daughter to the leader of the German Protestants, while the following year he began discussions with Catholic Spain to marry his son to the Infanta Maria. After some ten years of negotiations, James's hopes for what was known as the Spanish match were finally abandoned, much to the delight of the nation, whose long-felt fear and hatred for Spain outweighed the subtle political logic behind the plan.

But if James sought stability and peace, and for the most part succeeded in his aims (at least until 1618, when the bitter religio-political conflicts on the European continent swirled well out of the

King's control), he never really achieved concord and cohesion. He ruled over two kingdoms that did not know, like, or even want to understand one another, and his rule did little to bring them closer together. His England remained separate from his Scotland, even as he ruled over both. And even his England remained self divided, as in truth it always was under Elizabeth, ever more a nation of prosperity and influence but still one forged out of deep-rooted divisions of means, faiths, and allegiances that made the very nature of English identity a matter of confusion and concern. Arguably this is the very condition of great drama—sufficient peace and prosperity to support a theater industry and sufficient provocation in the troubling uncertainties about what the nation was and what fundamentally mattered to its people to inspire plays that would offer tentative solutions or at the very least make the troubling questions articulate and moving.

Nine years before James would die in 1625, Shakespeare died, having returned from London to the small market town in which he was born. If London, now a thriving modern metropolis of well over 200,000 people, had, like the nation itself, been transformed in the course of his life, the Warwickshire market town still was much the same. The house in which Shakespeare was born still stood, as did the church in which he was baptized and the school in which he learned to read and write. The river Avon still ran slowly along the town's southern limits. What had changed was that Shakespeare was now its most famous citizen, and, although it would take more than another 100 years to fully achieve this, he would in time become England's, for having turned the great ethical, social, and political issues of his own age into plays that would live forever.

William Shakespeare: A Chronology

1558	**November 17: Queen Elizabeth crowned**
1564	April 26: Shakespeare baptized, third child born to John Shakespeare and Mary Arden
1564	**May 27: Death of Jean Calvin in Geneva**
1565	John Shakespeare elected alderman in Stratford-upon-Avon
1568	**Publication of the Bishops' Bible**
1568	September 4: John Shakespeare elected Bailiff of Stratford-upon-Avon
1569	**Northern Rebellion**
1570	**Queen Elizabeth excommunicated by the Pope**
1572	**August 24: St. Bartholomew's Day Massacre in Paris**
1576	**The Theatre is built in Shoreditch**
1577–1580	**Sir Francis Drake sails around the world**
1582	November 27: Shakespeare and Anne Hathaway married (Shakespeare is 18)
1583	Queen's Men formed
1583	May 26: Shakespeare's daughter, Susanna, baptized
1584	**Failure of the Virginia Colony**

1585   February 2: Twins, Hamnet and Judith, baptized (Shakespeare is 20)

1586   **Babington Plot to dethrone Elizabeth and replace her with Mary, Queen of Scots**

1587   **February 8: Execution of Mary, Queen of Scots**

1587   **Rose Theatre built**

1588   **August: Defeat of the Spanish armada** (Shakespeare is 24)

1588   **September 4: Death of Robert Dudley, Earl of Leicester**

1590   **First three books of Spenser's *Faerie Queene* published; Marlowe's *Tamburlaine* published**

1592   March 3: *Henry VI, Part One* performed at the Rose Theatre (Shakespeare is 27)

1593   **February–November: Theaters closed because of plague**

1593   Publication of *Venus and Adonis*

1594   Publication of *Titus Andronicus*, first play by Shakespeare to appear in print (though anonymously)

1594   Lord Chamberlain's Men formed

1595   March 15: Payment made to Shakespeare, Will Kemp, and Richard Burbage for performances at court in December, 1594

1595   **Swan Theatre built**

1596   **Books 4–6 of *The Faerie Queene* published**

1596   August 11: Burial of Shakespeare's son, Hamnet (Shakespeare is 32)

1596–1599   Shakespeare living in St. Helen's, Bishopsgate, London

1596   October 20: Grant of Arms to John Shakespeare

1597   May 4: Shakespeare purchases New Place, one of the two largest houses in Stratford (Shakespeare is 33)

1598   Publication of *Love's Labor's Lost*, first extant play with Shakespeare's name on the title page

1598   Publication of Francis Meres's *Palladis Tamia*, citing Shakespeare as "the best for Comedy and Tragedy" among English writers

1599   Opening of the Globe Theatre

1601   February 7: Lord Chamberlain's Men paid 40 shillings to play *Richard II* by supporters of the Earl of Essex, the day before his abortive rebellion

1601   February 17: Execution of Robert Devereaux, Earl of Essex

1601   September 8: Burial of John Shakespeare

1602   May 1: Shakespeare buys 107 acres of farmland in Stratford

1603   March 24: Queen Elizabeth dies; James VI of Scotland succeeds as James I of England (Shakespeare is 39)

1603   May 19: Lord Chamberlain's Men reformed as the King's Men

1604   Shakespeare living with the Mountjoys, a French Huguenot family, in Cripplegate, London

1604   First edition of Marlowe's *Dr. Faustus* published (written c. 1589)

1604   March 15: Shakespeare named among "players" given scarlet cloth to wear at royal procession of King James

1604   Publication of authorized version of *Hamlet* (Shakespeare is 40)

1605   Gunpowder Plot

1605   June 5: Marriage of Susanna Shakespeare to John Hall

1608   Publication of *King Lear* (Shakespeare is 44)

1608–1609   Acquisition of indoor Blackfriars Theatre by King's Men

1609   *Sonnets* published

1611   King James Bible published (Shakespeare is 47)

1612   November 6: Death of Henry, eldest son of King James

1613   February 14: Marriage of King James's daughter Elizabeth to Frederick, the Elector Palatine

1613   March 10: Shakespeare, with some associates, buys gatehouse in Blackfriars, London

1613   June 29: Fire burns the Globe Theatre

1614   Rebuilt Globe reopens

1616   February 10: Marriage of Judith Shakespeare to Thomas Quiney

1616   March 25: Shakespeare's will signed

1616   April 23: Shakespeare dies (age 52)

1616   April 23: Cervantes dies in Madrid

1616   April 25: Shakespeare buried in Holy Trinity Church in Stratford-upon-Avon

1623   August 6: Death of Anne Shakespeare

1623   October: Prince Charles, King James's son, returns from Madrid, having failed to arrange his marriage to Maria Anna, Infanta of Spain

1623   First Folio published with 36 plays (18 never previously published)

Words, Words, Words: Understanding Shakespeare's Language
by David Scott Kastan

t is silly to pretend that it is easy to read Shakespeare. Reading Shakespeare isn't like picking up a copy of *USA Today* or *The New Yorker*, or even F. Scott Fitzgerald's *Great Gatsby* or Toni Morrison's *Beloved*. It is hard work, because the language is often unfamiliar to us and because it is more concentrated than we are used to. In the theater it is usually a bit easier. Actors can clarify meanings with gestures and actions, allowing us to get the general sense of what is going on, if not every nuance of the language that is spoken. "Action is eloquence," as Volumnia puts it in *Coriolanus*, "and the eyes of th' ignorant / More learnèd than the ears" (3.276–277). Yet the real greatness of Shakespeare rests not on "the general sense" of his plays but on the specificity and suggestiveness of the words in which they are written. It is through language that the plays' full dramatic power is realized, and it is that rich and robust language, often pushed by Shakespeare to the very limits of intelligibility, that we must learn to understand. But we can come to understand it (and enjoy it), and this essay is designed to help.

Even experienced readers and playgoers need help. They often find that his words are difficult to comprehend. Shakespeare sometimes uses words no longer current in English or with meanings that have changed. He regularly multiplies words where seemingly one might do as well or even better. He characteristically writes sentences that are syntactically complicated and imaginatively dense. And it isn't just we, removed by some 400 years from his world, who find him difficult to read; in his own time, his friends and fellow actors knew Shakespeare was hard. As two of them, John Hemings and Henry Condell, put it in their prefatory remarks to Shakespeare's First Folio in 1623, "read him, therefore, and again and again; and if then you do not like him, surely you are in some manifest danger not to understand him."

From the very beginning, then, it was obvious that the plays both deserve and demand not only careful reading but continued re-reading—and that not to read Shakespeare with all the attention a reader can bring to bear on the language is almost to guarantee that a reader will not "understand him" and remain among those who "do not like him." But Shakespeare's colleagues were nonetheless confident that the plays exerted an attraction strong enough to ensure and reward the concentration of their readers, confident, as they say, that in them "you will find enough, both to draw and hold you." The plays do exert a kind of magnetic pull, and have successfully drawn in and held readers for over 400 years.

Once we are drawn in, we confront a world of words that does not always immediately yield its delights; but it will—once we learn to see what is demanded of us. Words in Shakespeare do a lot, arguably more than anyone else has ever asked them to do. In part, it is because he needed his words to do many things at once. His stage had no sets and few props, so his words are all we have to enable us to imagine what his characters see. And they also allow us to see what the characters don't see, especially about themselves. The words are vivid and immediate, as well as complexly layered and psychologically suggestive. The difficulties they pose are not the "thee's" and "thou's" or "prithee's" and "doth's" that obviously mark the chronological distance between Shakespeare and us. When

Gertrude says to Hamlet, "thou hast thy father much offended" (3.4.8), we have no difficulty understanding her chiding, though we might miss that her use of the "thou" form of the pronoun expresses an intimacy that Hamlet pointedly refuses with his reply: "Mother, *you* have my father much offended" (3.4.9; italics mine).

Most deceptive are words that look the same as words we know but now mean something different. Words often change meanings over time. When Horatio and the soldiers try to stop Hamlet as he chases after the Ghost, Hamlet pushes past them and says, "I'll make a ghost of him that lets me" (1.4.85). It seems an odd thing to say. Why should he threaten someone who "lets" him do what he wants to do? But here "let" means "hinder," not, as it does today, "allow" (although the older meaning of the word still survives, for example, in tennis, where a "let serve" is one that is hindered by the net on its way across). There are many words that can, like this, mislead us: "his" sometimes means "its," "an" often means "if," "envy" means something more like "malice," "cousin" means more generally "kinsman," and there are others, though all are easily defined. The difficulty is that we may not stop to look thinking we already know what the word means, but in this edition a ° following the word alerts a reader that there is a gloss in the left margin, and quickly readers get used to these older meanings.

Then, of course, there is the intimidation factor—strange, polysyllabic, or Latinate words that not only are foreign to us but also must have sounded strange even to Shakespeare's audiences. When Macbeth wonders whether all the water in all the oceans of the world will be able to clean his bloody hands after the murder of Duncan, he concludes: "No; this my hand will rather / The multitudinous seas incarnadine, / Making the green one red" (2.2.64–66). Duncan's blood staining Macbeth's murderous hand is so offensive that, not merely does it resist being washed off in water, but it will "the multitudinous seas incarnadine": that is, turn the sea-green oceans blood-red. Notes will easily clarify the meaning of the two odd words, but it is worth observing that they would have been as odd to Shakespeare's readers as they are to us. The *Oxford English Dictionary* (*OED*) shows no use of "multitudinous" before this, and it records no use of "incarnadine" before 1591 (*Macbeth* was written about 1606). Both are new words, coined from the Latin, part of a process in Shakespeare's time where English adopted many Latinate words as a mark of its own emergence as an important vernacular language. Here they are used to express the magnitude of Macbeth's offense, a crime not only against the civil law but also against the cosmic order, and then the simple monosyllables of turning "the green one red" provide an immediate (and needed) paraphrase and register his own sickening awareness of the true hideousness of his deed.

As with "multitudinous" in *Macbeth*, Shakespeare is the source of a great many words in English. Sometimes he coined them himself, or, if he didn't invent them, he was the first person whose writing of them has survived. Some of these words have become part of our language, so common that it is hard to imagine they were not always part of it: for example, "assassination" (*Macbeth*, 1.7.2), "bedroom" (*A Midsummer Night's Dream*, 2.2.57), "countless" (*Titus Andronicus*, 5.3.59), "fashionable" (*Troilus and Cressida*, 3.3.165), "frugal" (*The Merry Wives of Windsor*, 2.1.28), "laughable" (*The Merchant of Venice*, 1.1.56), "lonely" (*Coriolanus*, 4.1.30), and "useful" (*King John*, 5.2.81). But other words that he originated were not as, to use yet another Shakespearean coinage, "successful" (*Titus Andronicus*, 1.1.66). Words like "crimeless" (*Henry VI, Part Two*, 2.4.63, meaning "innocent"), "facinorous" (*All's Well That Ends Well*, 2.3.30, meaning "extremely wicked"), and "recountment" (*As You Like It*, 4.3.141, meaning "narrative" or "account") have, without much resistance, slipped into oblivion. Clearly Shakespeare liked words, even unwieldy ones. His working vocabulary, about 18,000 words, is staggering, larger than almost any other English writer, and he seems to be the first person to use in print about

1,000 of these. Whether he coined the new words himself or was in-
trigued by the new words he heard in the streets of London doesn't
really matter; the point is that he was remarkably alert to and engaged with a dynamic language that was expanding in response to
England's own expanding contact with the world around it.

But it is neither new words nor old ones that are the source
of the greatest difficulty of Shakespeare's language. The real difficulty
(and the real delight) comes in trying to see how he uses the words,
how he endows them with more than their denotative meanings.
Why, for example, does Macbeth say that he hopes that the "sure and
firm-set earth" (2.1.56) will not hear his steps as he goes forward to
murder Duncan? Here "sure" and "firm-set" mean virtually the same
thing: stable, secure, fixed. Why use two words? If this were a student paper, no doubt the teacher would circle one of them and write
"redundant." But the redundancy is exactly what Shakespeare wants.
One word would do if the purpose were to describe the solidity of
the earth, but here the redundancy points to something different. It
reveals something about Macbeth's mind, betraying through the dou-
bling how deep is his awareness of the world of stable values that the
terrible act he is about to commit must unsettle.

Shakespeare's words usually work this way: in part describ-
ing what the characters see and as often betraying what they feel.
The example from *Macbeth* is a simple example of how this works.
Shakespeare's words are carefully patterned. How one says something is every bit as important as what is said, and the conspicuous
patterns that are created alert us to the fact that something more
than the words' lexical sense has been put into play. Words can be
coupled, as in the example above, or knit into even denser metaphori-
cal constellations to reveal something about the speaker (which often
the speaker does not know), as in Prince Hal's promise to his father
that he will outdo the rebels' hero, Henry Percy (Hotspur):

Percy is but my factor, good my lord,

To engross up glorious deeds on my behalf.

And I will call him to so strict account

That he shall render every glory up,

Yea, even the slightest worship of his time,

Or I will tear the reckoning from his heart.

(Henry IV, Part One, 3.2.147–152)

The Prince expresses his confidence that he will defeat Hotspur, but revealingly in a reiterated language of commercial exchange ("factor," "engross," "account," "render," "reckoning") that tells us something important both about the Prince and the ways in which he understands his world. In a play filled with references to coins and counterfeiting, the speech demonstrates not only that Hal has committed himself to the business at hand, repudiating his earlier, irresponsible tavern self, but also that he knows it is a business rather than a glorious world of chivalric achievement; he inhabits a world in which value (political as well as economic) is not intrinsic but determined by what people are willing to invest, and he proves himself a master of producing desire for what he has to offer.

Or sometimes it is not the network of imagery but the very syntax that speaks, as when Claudius announces his marriage to Hamlet's mother:

Therefore our sometime sister, now our Queen,

Th' imperial jointress to this warlike state,

Have we—as 'twere with a defeated joy,

With an auspicious and a dropping eye,

With mirth in funeral and with dole in marriage,

In equal scale weighing delight and dole—

Taken to wife.   *(Hamlet, 1.2.8–14)*

All he really wants to say here is that he has married Gertrude, his former sister-in-law: "Therefore our sometime sister . . . Have we . . . Taken to wife." But the straightforward sentence gets interrupted and complicated, revealing his own discomfort with the announcement. His elaborations and intensifications of Gertrude's role ("sometime sister," "Queen," "imperial jointress"), the self-conscious rhetorical balancing of the middle three lines (indeed "in equal scale weighing delight and dole"), all declare by the all-too obvious artifice how desperate he is to hide the awkward facts behind a veneer of normalcy and propriety. The very unnaturalness of the sentence is what alerts us that we are meant to understand more than the simple relation of fact.

Why doesn't Shakespeare just say what he means? Well, he does—exactly what he means. In the example from *Hamlet* just above, Shakespeare shows us something about Claudius that Claudius doesn't know himself. Always Shakespeare's words will offer us an immediate sense of what is happening, allowing us to follow the action, but they also offer us a counterplot, pointing us to what might be behind the action, confirming or contradicting what the characters say. It is a language that shimmers with promise and possibility, opening the characters' hearts and minds to our view—and all we have to do is learn to pay attention to what is there before us.

Shakespeare's Verse

Another distinctive feature of Shakespeare's dramatic language is that much of it is in verse. Almost all of the plays mix poetry and prose, but the poetry dominates. *The Merry Wives of Windsor* has the lowest percentage (only about 13 percent verse), while *Richard II* and *King John* are written entirely in verse (the only examples, although *Henry VI, Part One* and *Part Three* have only a very few prose lines). In most of the plays, about 70 percent of the lines are written in verse.

Shakespeare's characteristic verse line is a non-rhyming iambic pentameter ("blank verse"), ten syllables with every second one stressed. In *A Midsummer Night's Dream*, Titania comes to her senses after a magic potion has led her to fall in love with an ass-headed Bottom: "Methought I was enamored of an ass" (4.1.76). Similarly, in *Romeo and Juliet*, Romeo gazes up at Juliet's window: "But soft, what light through yonder window breaks" (2.2.2). In both these examples, the line has ten syllables organized into five regular beats (each beat consisting of the stress on the second syllable of a pair, as in "But soft," the da-dum rhythm forming an "iamb"). Still, we don't hear these lines as jingles; they seem natural enough, in large part because this dominant pattern is varied in the surrounding lines.

The play of stresses indeed becomes another key to meaning, as Shakespeare alerts us to what is important. In *Measure for Measure*, Lucio urges Isabella to plead for her brother's life: "Oh, to him, to him, wench! He will relent" (2.2.129). The iambic norm (unstressed-stressed) tells us (and an actor) that the emphasis at the beginning of the line is on "to" not "him"—it is the action not the object that is being emphasized—and at the end of the line the stress falls on "will." Alternatively, the line can play against the established norm. In *Hamlet*, Claudius corrects Polonius's idea of what is bothering the Prince: "Love? His affections do not that way tend" (3.1.161). The iambic norm forces the emphasis onto "that" ("do not *that* way tend"), while the syntax forces an unexpected stress on the opening word, "Love." In the famous line, "The course of true love never did run smooth" (*A Midsummer Night's Dream*, 1.1.134), the iambic expectation is varied in both the middle and at the end of the line. Both "love" and the first syllable of "never" are stressed, as are both syllables at the end: "run smooth," creating a metrical foot in which both syllables are stressed (called a "spondee"). The point to notice is that the "da-dum, da-dum, da-dum, da-dum, da-dum" line is not inevitable; it merely sets an expectation against which many variations can be heard.

In fact, even the ten-syllable norm can be varied. Shakespeare sometimes writes lines with fewer or more syllables. Often there is an extra, unstressed syllable at the end of a line (a so-called "feminine ending"); sometimes there are verse lines with only nine. In *Henry IV, Part One*, King Henry replies incredulously to the rebel Worcester's claim that he hadn't "sought" the confrontation with the King: "You have not sought it. How comes it then?" (5.1.27). There are only nine syllables here (some earlier editors, seeking to "correct" the verse, added the word "sir" after the first question to regularize the line). But the pause where one expects a stressed syllable is dramatically effective, allowing the King's anger to be powerfully present in the silence.

As even these few examples show, Shakespeare's verse is unusually flexible, allowing a range of rhythmical effects. It should not be understood as a set of strict rules but as a flexible set of practices rooted in dramatic necessity. It is designed to highlight ideas and emotions, and it is based less upon rigid syllable counts than on an arrangement of stresses within an understood temporal norm, as one might expect from a poetry written to be heard in the theater rather than read on the page.

Here Follows Prose

Although the plays are dominated by verse, prose plays a significant role. Shakespeare's prose has its own rhythms, but it lacks the formal patterning of verse, and so is printed without line breaks and without the capitals that mark the beginning of a verse line. Like many of his fellow dramatists, Shakespeare tended to use prose for comic scenes, the shift from verse serving, especially in his early plays, as a social marker. Upper-class characters speak in verse; lower-class characters speak in prose. Thus, in *A Midsummer Night's Dream*, the Athenians of the court, as well as the fairies, all speak in verse, but the "rude mechanicals," Bottom and his artisan friends, all speak in prose, except for the comic verse they speak in their performance of "Pyramis and Thisbe."

As Shakespeare grew in experience, he became more flexible about the shifts from verse to prose, letting it, among other things, mark genre rather than class and measure various kinds of intensity. Prose becomes in the main the medium of comedy. The great comedies, like *Much Ado About Nothing*, *Twelfth Night*, and *As You Like It*, are all more than 50 percent prose. But even in comedy, shifts between verse and prose may be used to measure subtle emotional changes. In Act One, scene three of *The Merchant of Venice*, Shylock and Bassanio begin the scene speaking of matters of business in prose, but when Antonio enters and the deep conflict between the Christian and the Jew becomes evident, the scene shifts to verse. But prose may itself serve in moments of emotional intensity. Shylock's famous speech in Act Three, scene one, "Hath not a Jew eyes . . ." is all in prose, as is Hamlet's expression of disgust at the world ("I have of late— but wherefore I know not—lost all my mirth . . .") at 3.1.261–276. Shakespeare comes to use prose to vary the tone of a scene, as the shift from verse subtly alerts an audience or a reader to some new emotional register.

Prose becomes, as Shakespeare's art matures, not inevitably the mark of the lower classes but the mark of a salutary daily-ness. It is appropriately the medium in which letters are written, and it is the medium of a common sense that will at least challenge the potential self-deceptions of grandiloquent speech. When Rosalind mocks the excesses and artifice of Orlando's wooing in Act Four, scene one of *As You Like It*, it is in prose that she seeks something genuine in the expression of love:

The poor world is almost six thousand years old, and in all this time there was not any man died in his own person, *videlicit* [i.e., namely], in a love cause. . . . Men have died from time to time, and worms have eaten them, but not for love.

Here the prose becomes the sound of common sense, an effective foil to the affectation of pinning poems to trees and thinking that it is real love.

It is not that prose is artless; Shakespeare's prose is no less self-conscious than his verse. The artfulness of his prose is different, of course. The seeming ordinariness of his prose is no less an effect of his artistry than is the more obvious patterning of his verse. Prose is no less serious, compressed, or indeed figurative. As with his verse, Shakespeare's prose performs numerous tasks and displays various, subtle formal qualities; and recognizing the possibilities of what it can achieve is still another way of seeing what Shakespeare puts right before us to show us what he has hidden.

Further Reading

N.F. Blake, *Shakespeare's Language: An Introduction* (New York: St. Martin's Press, 1983).

Jonathan Hope, *Shakespeare's Grammar* (London: Thomson, 2003).

Sister Miriam Joseph, *Shakespeare's Use of the Arts of Language* (New York: Columbia University Press, 1947).

M. M. Mahood, *Shakespeare's Wordplay* (London: Methuen, 1957).

Russ McDonald, *Shakespeare and the Arts of Language* (Oxford: Oxford University Press, 2001).

Brian Vickers, *The Artistry of Shakespeare's Prose* (London: Methuen, 1968).

George T. Wright, *Shakespeare's Metrical Art* (Berkeley: Univ. of California Press, 1991).

Key to the Play Text

Symbols

°	Indicates an explanation or definition in the left-hand margin.
¹	Indicates a gloss on the page facing the play text.
[ ]	Indicates something added or changed by the editors (i.e., not in the early printed text that this edition of the play is based on).

Terms

F, *Folio*, or *First Folio*	The first collected edition of Shakespeare's plays, published in 1623, and the basis for this edition (see Editing *Julius Caesar*, page 287).

Julius Caesar

William Shakespeare

List of Roles

Julius Caesar
Calphurnia   *his wife*
Servant
Ghost of Caesar

Marcus Brutus
Portia   *his wife*
Lucius   *their servant*

Mark Antony
Octavius Caesar   } *triumvirs after Caesar's death*
M. Aemilius Lepidus
Servant   *to Mark Antony*

Caius Cassius
Casca
Cinna
Decius Brutus   *conspirators against Julius Caesar*
Metellus Cimber
Caius Ligarius
Trebonius

Cicero
Publius   } *Senators*
Popilius Lena

Flavius
Murellus   } *tribunes*

Lucilius
Titinius
Messala   *soldiers and supporters*
Cato   *of Brutus and Cassius*
Volumnius

Strato
Varrus
Claudio   *soldiers and supporters*
Clitus   *of Brutus and Cassius*
Dardanius
Labio Flavius
Pindarus   *Cassius's servant*

Artemidorus
Cinna the Poet
Carpenter
Cobbler
Soothsayer
Plebeians (Commoners)
Servants
Soldiers
Messengers

Senators, commoners, servants, soldiers, attendants

1 **Flavius, Murellus**

Flavius and Murellus are *tribunes*, the elected representatives of the commoners (or *plebeians*) whose task was to negotiate on their behalf with the other organs of government in republican Rome, principally the Senate and the consuls. (See LONGER NOTE, page 283.)

2 *holiday*

The word derives from *holy days*, saints' days when reveling and carnival broke up the daily rhythms of life. After the Reformation, holidays were often associated with Catholicism, as Protestants complained about the ways in which they seduced the populace away from the serious issues of work and devotion. Here, the commoners are, as Murellus later points out, celebrating a triumph over other Romans in the civil wars that propelled Caesar to unrivalled power, not, as they seem to imagine, victory over a foreign power that expanded the empire and brought back to Rome the spoils of war. Such events were celebrated by spectacular parades into the city itself (*triumphs*) when the victorious general would lead

his army into the city with captives and treasures in tow. Caesar, one of Rome's most successful generals, had many such triumphs after his spectacular victories in Gaul and Spain. Flavius's words are designed to contrast Caesar's triumphs in the service of Rome to those that have occurred at the expense of Rome's own citizens.

3 *without the sign / Of your profession*

Without wearing the garments or carrying the tools of your trade

4 *in respect of*

When compared to

5 *cobbler*

Both "shoemaker" and "bungler" (clumsy, unskillful worker)

6 *Answer me directly.*

Give me a straight answer.

7 *soles*

The *soles* of shoes; also a pun on "souls"

8 *if you be out, sir, I can mend you*

If you be out of sorts, i.e., angry, I can fix that (and also: If your soles are worn out, I can fix them).

Act 1, Scene 1

Enter **Flavius**, **Murellus**, [1] [*a* **Carpenter**, *a* **Cobbler**,] *and certain* [*other*] **Commoners** *over the stage.*

Flavius

Hence! Home, you idle creatures; get you home!

Is this a holiday? [2] What, know you not,

tradesmen Being mechanical,° you ought not walk

Upon a laboring day without the sign

Of your profession? [3]—Speak, what trade art thou?   5

Carpenter

Why, sir, a carpenter.

Murellus

ruler Where is thy leather apron and thy rule?°

What dost thou with thy best apparel on?

—You, sir, what trade are you?

Cobbler

Truly, sir, in respect of [4] a fine workman, I am but, as   10

you would say, a cobbler. [5]

Murellus

But what trade art thou? Answer me directly. [6]

Cobbler

A trade, sir, that I hope I may use with a safe con-

science, which is, indeed, sir, a mender of bad soles. [7]

Murellus

rogue / worthless What trade, thou knave?° Thou naughty° knave, what

trade?   15

Cobbler

angry Nay, I beseech you, sir, be not out° with me. Yet, if you

be out, sir, I can mend you. [8]

Murellus

What mean'st thou by that? "Mend" me, thou saucy fellow?

1   *cobble you*
    Both "fix your shoes" and "hit
    you with stones"

2   *all that I live by is with the awl*
    I make my complete living with an
    awl (a small pointed tool used to
    pierce holes in leather)

3   *withal*
    Nevertheless; also a pun on "with awl"

4   *recover*
    Resole; also a pun meaning
    "rescue" or "restore"

5   *As proper men as ever trod upon neat's
    leather have gone upon my handiwork.*
    I.e., I have made shoes for the finest
    men.

6   *triumph*
    Official triumphal procession. The
    triumph referred to here celebrates
    Caesar's victory in the battle of
    Munda, in which he defeated the
    army led by the sons of Pompey the
    Great, Caesar's former ally and
    subsequent rival for power in
    Rome.

7   *What conquest brings he home?*
    Murellus reminds the commoners
    that Caesar had been fighting
    against their fellow Romans, not
    conquering new lands (i.e.,
    bringing home conquests).

8   *What tributaries follow him to Rome / To
    grace in captive bonds his chariot wheels?*
    In ancient Rome, captives often
    were tied to the conqueror's
    chariot and paraded through the
    city as spoils of war.

9   *Pompey*
    Pompey the Great (106–48 B.C.) was
    another great Roman general and a
    rival to Julius Caesar. Like Caesar, he
    enjoyed long periods of popularity
    for his victories in the service of
    Rome. As Rome's republican
    institutions began to decay and
    could no longer control the rising
    force of the military, Pompey formed
    a triumvirate with Caesar and
    Crassus, one which proved as
    unstable as all such alliances (see
    note to 4.1.1). Pompey, perhaps
    inaccurately, was associated with
    the defense of the Republic, as
    Murellus's comments here
    demonstrate. Pompey opposed
    Caesar rather late in the day, having
    failed to take his rival seriously
    enough. He was decisively defeated
    at the battle of Pharsalia in August
    48, before he fled to Egypt, where he
    was murdered as he sought asylum.
    Shakespeare has telescoped events
    here for dramatic effect, as Pompey's
    death was four years before that of
    Caesar. Shakespeare's treatment
    may owe something to Lucan's (A.D.
    39–65) great epic of the civil wars,
    the *Pharsalia*, which is much more
    sympathetic to the defeated Pompey
    than to the triumphant Caesar.

Cobbler

Why, sir, cobble you. [1]

Flavius

Thou art a cobbler, art thou?   20

Cobbler

Truly, sir, all that I live by is with the awl. [2] I meddle with no
tradesman's matters nor women's matters, but withal [3] I
am indeed, sir, a surgeon to old shoes. When they are in
great danger, I recover [4] them. As proper men as ever trod

cow's   upon neat's° leather have gone upon my handiwork. [5]   25

Flavius

why   But wherefore° art not in thy shop today?

Why dost thou lead these men about the streets?

Cobbler

Truly, sir, to wear out their shoes to get myself into
more work. But indeed, sir, we make holiday to see
Caesar and to rejoice in his triumph. [6]   30

Murellus

Wherefore rejoice? What conquest brings he home? [7]

tribute (ransom) payers   What tributaries° follow him to Rome

To grace in captive bonds his chariot wheels? [8]

i.e., unfeeling   You blocks, you stones, you worse than senseless° things,

O you hard hearts, you cruel men of Rome,   35

Knew you not Pompey? [9] Many a time and oft

Have you climbed up to walls and battlements,

To towers and windows, yea, to chimney tops,

Your infants in your arms, and there have sat

The livelong day with patient expectation   40

To see great Pompey pass the streets of Rome.

merely   And when you saw his chariot but° appear,

Have you not made an universal shout

(Rome's Tiber River)   That Tiber° trembled underneath her banks

echo   To hear the replication° of your sounds   45

1   *That needs must light on this ingratitude*
    **That will inevitably come as
    punishment for your ungrateful
    behavior**

2   *till the lowest stream / Do kiss the most
    exalted shores of all*
    **Until (your tears) raise the river at
    its lowest level to its highest banks**

3   *whe'er their basest mettle be not moved*
    **Whether the most vulgar among
    them is not emotionally stirred**

4   *Capitol*
    **Capitoline Hill, where the temple
    of Jupiter was located**

5   *decked with ceremonies*
    **Adorned with ceremonial scarves (see
    1.2.287); the *trophies* of line 68**

6   *feast of Lupercal*
    **Festival held on February 15 to
    honor Lupercus, the god of fertility
    and agriculture (equivalent to the
    Greek god Pan)**

7   *These growing feathers plucked from Cae-
    sar's wing / Will make him fly an ordinary
    pitch*
    **I.e., if we remove Caesar's popular
    support his power will remain
    within normal boundaries.**

Made in her concave shores?

And do you now put on your best attire?

pick And do you now cull° out a holiday?

And do you now strew flowers in his way

children That comes in triumph over Pompey's blood?° 50

Be gone!

Run to your houses, fall upon your knees,

prevent Pray to the gods to intermit° the plague

That needs must light on this ingratitude. **1**

Flavius

Go, go, good countrymen, and for this fault 55

rank Assemble all the poor men of your sort,°

Draw them to Tiber banks, and weep your tears

Into the channel till the lowest stream

Do kiss the most exalted shores of all. **2**

All the **Commoners** *exit.*

See whe'er their basest mettle be not moved; **3** 60

They vanish tongue-tied in their guiltiness.

Go you down that way towards the Capitol; **4**

statues This way will I. Disrobe the images°

If you do find them decked with ceremonies. **5**

Murellus

May we do so? 65

You know it is the feast of Lupercal. **6**

Flavius

It is no matter. Let no images

walk around Be hung with Caesar's trophies. I'll about°

commoners And drive away the vulgar° from the streets.

gathered in groups So do you too, where you perceive them thick.° 70

These growing feathers plucked from Caesar's wing

Will make him fly an ordinary pitch, **7**

otherwise Who else° would soar above the view of men

And keep us all in servile fearfulness.

They exit [separately].

1   [dressed] for the course

**As part of the Lupercalia, young
men dressed in goatskins ran a
race (*course*) around the Palatine,
the hill where the twins Romulus
and Remus, the founders of Rome,
were believed to have been
suckled by a she-wolf.**

2   *The barren, touchèd in this holy chase, /
Shake off their sterile curse*

**As part of the Lupercalia, the young
men running the course would
lash the people they met—
particularly women—with strips of
goatskin, in the belief that it would
help promote fertility.**

3   Sennet

**Trumpet flourish (as in stage
direction following line 26)**

Act 1, Scene 2

[*Flourish.*] *Enter* **Caesar**, **Antony** [*dressed*] *for the course,* [1]
Calphurnia, **Portia**, **Decius**, **Cicero**, **Brutus**, **Cassius**,
Casca, [*and*] *a* **Soothsayer** [*in a throng of* **Commoners**];
after them, **Murellus** *and* **Flavius**.

Caesar
Calphurnia.
Casca
Peace, ho! Caesar speaks!
Caesar
Calphurnia!
Calphurnia
Here, my lord.
Caesar
Stand you directly in Antonio's way   5
When he doth run his course.—Antonio!
Antony
Caesar, my lord?
Caesar
Forget not in your speed, Antonio,
To touch Calphurnia, for our elders say
The barren, touchèd in this holy chase,   10
Shake off their sterile curse. [2]
Antony
                                          I shall remember:
When Caesar says, "do this," it is performed.
Caesar
Continue   Set° on and leave no ceremony out.   [*Sennet*] [3]
Soothsayer
Caesar!

49

1   *Caesar is turned to hear.*

You have my full attention.

2   *ides of March*

The 15th of March. See LONGER
NOTE, page 283.

3   *Pass!*

Let us move onward.

Caesar

Ha! Who calls? 15

Casca

Bid every noise be still. Peace yet again.

Caesar

crowd Who is it in the press° that calls on me?

I hear a tongue, shriller than all the music,

Cry "Caesar!"—Speak. Caesar is turned to hear. [1]

Soothsayer

Beware the ides of March. [2]

Caesar

What man is that? 20

Brutus

A soothsayer bids you beware the ides of March.

Caesar

Set him before me. Let me see his face.

Cassius

Fellow, come from the throng. Look upon Caesar.

Caesar

What say'st thou to me now? Speak once again.

Soothsayer

Beware the ides of March. 25

Caesar

He is a dreamer. Let us leave him. Pass! [3]

Sennet. All except **Brutus** *and* **Cassius** *exit.*

Cassius

running Will you go see the order° of the course?

Brutus

Not I.

Cassius

I pray you, do.

1   *of late*

     Lately

2   *You bear too stubborn and too strange a*
     hand / Over your friend that loves you.

     I.e., you are too harsh and
     unsympathetic to me. (The
     metaphor *bear . . . a hand* **comes**
     from horseback riding, referring to
     the rider's control of the reins.)

3   *If I have veiled my look, / I turn the trouble*
     of my countenance / Merely upon myself.

     If I have seemed distant it is only
     because I am preoccupied with my
     own concerns.

4   *Vexèd I am / Of late with passions of*
     some difference, / Conceptions only
     proper to myself

     Lately I have been troubled by
     conflicting emotions, which are
     merely private matters.

5   *Nor construe any further my neglect*

     Nor interpret my neglect as
     anything more

6   *mistook your passion, / By means whereof*

     Misunderstood your feelings, and
     as a consequence

Brutus

playful   I am not gamesome.° I do lack some part   30
lively   Of that quick° spirit that is in Antony.
           Let me not hinder, Cassius, your desires.
           I'll leave you.

Cassius

           Brutus, I do observe you now of late. [1]
           I have not from your eyes that gentleness   35
accustomed And show of love as I was wont° to have.
           You bear too stubborn and too strange a hand
           Over your friend that loves you. [2]

Brutus

                                          Cassius,
           Be not deceived. If I have veiled my look,
           I turn the trouble of my countenance   40
Entirely   Merely° upon myself. [3] Vexèd I am
           Of late with passions of some difference,
           Conceptions only proper to myself, [4]
blemish   Which give some soil° perhaps to my behaviors.
           But let not therefore my good friends be grieved—   45
           Among which number, Cassius, be you one—
           Nor construe any further my neglect [5]
           Than that poor Brutus, with himself at war,
           Forgets the shows of love to other men.

Cassius

           Then, Brutus, I have much mistook your passion,   50
           By means whereof [6] this breast of mine hath buried
           Thoughts of great value, worthy cogitations.
           Tell me, good Brutus, can you see your face?

Brutus

           No, Cassius, for the eye sees not itself
Except   But° by reflection, by some other things.   55

1　*mirrors as will turn / Your hidden worthiness into your eye*

Mirrors that might reveal to you your own hidden value

2　*immortal Caesar*

Cassius is being ironic here (see lines 99–133), pointing at the cult of adoration that has formed around Caesar.

3　*groaning underneath this age's yoke*

Suffering under the burdens of these times

4　*that noble Brutus had his eyes*

That Brutus could see the situation through *his* (the hypothetical Roman's) *eyes*

5　*Therefore*

Cassius ignores Brutus's concern, continuing with his own thought (though some editors take *Therefore* to mean "as for that").

6　*jealous on*

Suspicious of

7　*did use / To stale with ordinary oaths my love / To every new protester*

Were accustomed to cheapening my friendship by declaring my devotion to every man who professed his friendship to me

8　*profess myself in banqueting / To all the rout*

While carousing, declare my friendship to all the rabble

Cassius

true   'Tis just.°

And it is very much lamented, Brutus,

That you have no such mirrors as will turn

Your hidden worthiness into your eye [1]

image   That you might see your shadow.° I have heard   60

reputation   Where many of the best respect° in Rome,

Except immortal Caesar, [2] speaking of Brutus

And groaning underneath this age's yoke, [3]

Have wished that noble Brutus had his eyes. [4]

Brutus

Into what dangers would you lead me, Cassius,   65

That you would have me seek into myself

For that which is not in me?

Cassius

Therefore, [5] good Brutus, be prepared to hear,

And, since you know you cannot see yourself

mirror   So well as by reflection, I, your glass,°   70

reveal   Will modestly discover° to yourself

i.e., aspect of That of° yourself which you yet know not of.

noble   And be not jealous on [6] me, gentle° Brutus.

laughingstock Were I a common laughter,° or did use

cheapen   To stale° with ordinary oaths my love   75

To every new protester; [7] if you know

That I do fawn on men and hug them hard

slander   And, after, scandal° them, or if you know

That I profess myself in banqueting

consider   To all the rout, [8] then hold° me dangerous.   80

Flourish, and shout.

Brutus

What means this shouting? I do fear the people

Choose Caesar for their king.

1 *Set honor in one eye and death i' th' other*

   **Set the promise of honor against
   the threat of death**

2 *so speed me as I love*

   **Make me successful, as long as I
   love**

3 *virtue*

   **I.e., honor; but the idea of civic
   virtue, a commitment to *the general
   good* (line 87), was one of the central
   tenets of a republican ideology.**

4 *I had as lief not be as live to be / In awe of
   such a thing as I myself*

   **I would as gladly die as to be
   subordinate to a man no better
   than myself (i.e., Caesar)**

5 *chafing with*

   Beating against

6 *lusty sinews*

   **I.e., strong muscles (though *sinews*
   literally means "tendons")**

7 *throwing it aside / And stemming it with
   hearts of controversy*

   **i.e., Confronting the angry waters
   with our competitive natures
   (directed both toward the tide and
   toward each other)**

Cassius

Ay, do you fear it?

Then must I think you would not have it so.

Brutus

I would not, Cassius, yet I love him well.

why But wherefore° do you hold me here so long? 85

What is it that you would impart to me?

anything If it be aught° toward the general good,

Set honor in one eye and death i' th' other, [1]

impartially And I will look on both indifferently,°

For let the gods so speed me as I love [2] 90

The name of honor more than I fear death.

Cassius

I know that virtue [3] to be in you, Brutus,

appearance As well as I do know your outward favor.°

Well, honor is the subject of my story.

I cannot tell what you and other men 95

Think of this life, but, for my single self,

gladly I had as lief° not be as live to be

In awe of such a thing as I myself. [4]

I was born free as Caesar. So were you.

We both have fed as well, and we can both 100

Endure the winter's cold as well as he.

For once upon a raw and gusty day,

The troubled Tiber chafing with [5] her shores,

Caesar said to me, "Dar'st thou, Cassius, now

sea Leap in with me into this angry flood° 105

And swim to yonder point?" Upon the word,

Dressed Accoutred° as I was, I plungèd in

And bade him follow. So indeed he did.

The torrent roared, and we did buffet it

With lusty sinews, [6] throwing it aside 110

And stemming it with hearts of controversy. [7]

1   *the point proposed*

   At our agreed destination

2   *Aeneas, our great ancestor, / Did from*
   the flames of Troy upon his shoulder /
   The old Anchises bear

   Escaping the burning Troy, the
   Trojan hero Aeneas carried his
   father, Anchises, to safety. In
   Virgil's Latin epic, *The Aeneid*,
   Aeneas's wanderings eventually
   led to the founding of Rome.

3   *bend his body*

   Bow

4   *the fit*

   I.e., epilepsy (see line 255 and
   note)

5   *His coward lips did from their color fly*

   I.e., Caesar's cowardly lips turned
   pale (but *color* also suggests
   military colors, or flags, making
   the image one of desertion)

6   *get the start of*

   Have the primary position in

7   *Colossus*

   An enormous bronze statue of the
   Roman god Apollo, now destroyed,
   which straddled the harbor at
   Rhodes and was one of the seven
   wonders of the ancient world.

But ere we could arrive the point proposed, [1]
Caesar cried, "Help me, Cassius, or I sink!"
I, as Aeneas, our great ancestor,
Did from the flames of Troy upon his shoulder   115
The old Anchises bear, [2] so from the waves of Tiber
Did I the tired Caesar. And this man
Is now become a god, and Cassius is
A wretched creature and must bend his body [3]
casually   If Caesar carelessly° but nod on him.   120
He had a fever when he was in Spain,
And, when the fit [4] was on him, I did mark
How he did shake. 'Tis true; this god did shake!
His coward lips did from their color fly, [5]
gaze   And that same eye whose bend° doth awe the world   125
its   Did lose his° luster. I did hear him groan,
Ay, and that tongue of his, that bade the Romans
Pay attention to   Mark° him and write his speeches in their books,
(a friend of Cassius)   "Alas," it cried, "give me some drink, Titinius,"°
As a sick girl. Ye gods, it doth amaze me   130
constitution   A man of such a feeble temper° should
So get the start of [6] the majestic world
(sign of victory)   And bear the palm° alone.   *Shout. Flourish.*

Brutus
                              Another general shout!
I do believe that these applauses are
For some new honors that are heaped on Caesar.   135

Cassius
straddle   Why, man, he doth bestride° the narrow world
Like a Colossus, [7] and we petty men
Walk under his huge legs and peep about
To find ourselves dishonorable graves.
Men at some time are masters of their fates.   140

1   *not in our stars*

Not determined by the influence of the stars

2   *Conjure with 'em*

Speak them aloud as spells to raise the dead (though in fact neither name will have any effect)

3   *the great flood*

A flood sent by Zeus, which killed all humans except the virtuous Deucalion and his wife, Pyrrha. This Greek myth (with a Roman analogue) is similar to the biblical story of Noah.

4   *When went there by an age since the great flood / But it was famed with more than with one man?*

Since the time of the flood, has there been any era that was celebrated only for one great man?

5   *When could they say till now, that talked of Rome*

Until now, how could anyone, when speaking of Rome, have ever said

6   *Rome indeed, and room enough*

***Rome* and *room* were pronounced similarly in Shakespeare's time.**

7   *a Brutus once*

Lucius Junius Brutus, founder of the Roman Republic and famed for defeating the Tarquins and ending the monarchy in Rome (509 B.C.)

8   *would have brooked / Th' eternal devil to keep his state in Rome / As easily as a king*

I.e., would no more tolerate the *devil* ruling in Rome than a king

9   *I am nothing jealous*

I do not doubt

10   *What you would work me to, I have some aim.*

I have some idea what you would incite me to do.

The fault, dear Brutus, is not in our stars [1]

subordinates   But in ourselves that we are underlings.°

Brutus and Caesar—what should be in that "Caesar"?

celebrated   Why should that name be sounded° more than yours?

Write them together: yours is as fair a name.   145

Speak   Sound° them: it doth become the mouth as well.

Weigh them: it is as heavy. Conjure with 'em: [2]

raise   "Brutus" will start° a spirit as soon as "Caesar."

Now in the names of all the gods at once,

food   Upon what meat° doth this our Caesar feed   150

i.e., The present era   That he is grown so great? Age,° thou art shamed!

Rome, thou hast lost the breed of noble bloods!

When went there by an age since the great flood [3]

But it was famed with more than with one man? [4]

When could they say till now, that talked of Rome, [5]   155

That her wide walks encompassed but one man?

Now is it Rome indeed, and room enough, [6]

When there is in it but one only man.

Oh, you and I have heard our fathers say

tolerated   There was a Brutus once [7] that would have brooked°   160

Th' eternal devil to keep his state in Rome

As easily as a king. [8]

Brutus

That you do love me, I am nothing jealous. [9]

What you would work me to, I have some aim. [10]

How I have thought of this and of these times   165

moment   I shall recount hereafter. For this present,°

I would not, so with love I might entreat you,

urged   Be any further moved.° What you have said

I will consider; what you have to say

I will with patience hear and find a time   170

fitting / important   Both meet° to hear and answer such high° things.

1   *Than to repute himself a son of Rome*

Than consider myself a Roman
citizen

2   *Cicero*

Marcus Tullius Cicero (106–43 B.C.)
was one of the most important
public figures of the Roman
Republic in the eyes of the
Elizabethans. His work was studied
by everyone who had an education,
and he was generally known by the
affectionate name of Tully. As a
philosopher and statesman, Cicero
played a major role in Roman life,
attempting to express the spirit of
its institutions and its culture of
public debate. As the Republic
declined, he wrote a major defense
of its constitution and an
influential work on the value of
friendship, doing all he could to
defend the Republic from its
enemies by preserving its ideals of
balance and equality. He also
wrote a series of letters that further
expressed his great faith in
republican ideals. Cicero was
usually adept at staying out of
trouble and not taking sides, which
led some to see him as an impartial
and honorable figure, others as
cautious and self-serving. He was
eventually murdered by Antony and
Octavius (as reported in this play at
4.3.179–180), who were afraid that he
might help rally the republican cause
they were eager to crush.

think   Till then, my noble friend, chew° upon this:
             Brutus had rather be a villager
             Than to repute himself a son of Rome[1]
             Under these hard conditions as this time   175
likely   Is like° to lay upon us.

Cassius

                        I am glad
even   That my weak words have struck but° thus much show
             Of fire from Brutus.

followers   Enter **Caesar** *and his train*° [*including* **Casca**].

Brutus

             The games are done, and Caesar is returning.

Cassius

             As they pass by, pluck Casca by the sleeve,   180
             And he will, after his sour fashion, tell you
that is worthy of   What hath proceeded worthy° note today.

Brutus

             I will do so. But, look you, Cassius,
             The angry spot doth glow on Caesar's brow,
scolded   And all the rest look like a chidden° train: 185
             Calphurnia's cheek is pale, and Cicero[2]
i.e., red Looks with such ferret° and such fiery eyes
             As we have seen him in the Capitol
opposed / debate   Being crossed° in conference° by some senators.

Cassius

             Casca will tell us what the matter is.   190

Caesar

             Antonio.

Antony

             Caesar.

1   *Yond Cassius*

Cassius over there

2   *Yet if my name were liable to fear*

But if I were subject to fear. Caesar insists that he is beyond such weakness.

3   *he looks / Quite through the deeds of men*

He can see in men's actions the hidden motives behind them.

4   *hears no music*

Not to enjoy music suggested the listener's own lack of harmony. See *The Merchant of Venice*, 5.1.92–94: "The man who hath no music in himself . . . Is fit for treasons, stratagems, and spoils."

5   *I rather tell thee what is to be feared / Than what I fear*

I am telling you what ought to be feared, rather than anything I fear myself.

Caesar

Let me have men about me that are fat,

Sleek-headed men and such as sleep a-nights.

Yond Cassius[1] has a lean and hungry look.   195

He thinks too much. Such men are dangerous.

Antony

Fear him not, Caesar. He's not dangerous.

disposed   He is a noble Roman and well given.°

Caesar

I wish   Would° he were fatter! But I fear him not.

Yet if my name were liable to fear,[2]   200

I do not know the man I should avoid

lean   So soon as that spare° Cassius. He reads much,

He is a great observer, and he looks

Quite through the deeds of men.[3] He loves no plays,

As thou dost, Antony. He hears no music.[4]   205

manner   Seldom he smiles, and smiles in such a sort°

As if he mocked himself and scorned his spirit

That could be moved to smile at anything.

Such men as he be never at heart's ease

one   Whiles they behold a° greater than themselves,   210

And therefore are they very dangerous.

I rather tell thee what is to be feared

Than what I fear,[5] for always I am Caesar.

side   Come on my right hand,° for this ear is deaf,

And tell me truly what thou think'st of him.   215

               Sennet. **Caesar** *and his train [except* **Casca***] exit.*

Casca

[*to* **Brutus**] You pulled me by the cloak. Would you

speak with me?

Brutus

happened   Aye, Casca. Tell us what hath chanced° today

somber; serious   That Caesar looks so sad.°

1   *put it by*

    Refused it

2   *marry*

    **Indeed. A mild oath derived from
    the phrase "by the Virgin Mary."**

Casca

Why? You were with him, were you not?   220

Brutus

happened I should not then ask, Casca, what had chanced.°

Casca

Why, there was a crown offered him, and, being
offered him, he put it by[1] with the back of his hand,
thus; and then the people fell a-shouting.

Brutus

What was the second noise for?   225

Casca

Why, for that too.

Cassius

They shouted thrice. What was the last cry for?

Casca

Why, for that too.

Brutus

Was the crown offered him thrice?

Casca

Ay, marry,[2] was 't, and he put it by thrice, every time   230
the other gentler than other,° and at every putting-by mine
honest neighbors shouted.

Cassius

Who offered him the crown?

Casca

Why, Antony.

Brutus

noble Tell us the manner of it, gentle° Casca.   235

Casca

I can as well be hanged as tell the manner of it. It was
complete / pay attention to mere° foolery. I did not mark° it.

1   *coronets*

Small crowns (wreathed with laurel branches, according to Plutarch, Shakespeare's major source for the Roman history, which he would have read in Thomas North's 1575 English translation)

2   *'Tis very like. He hath the falling sickness.*

It is not surprising. He has epilepsy. Plutarch reports that Caesar was "subject . . . to the falling sickness."

3   *we have the falling sickness*

I.e., our fortunes fall (as Caesar's rise).

4   *came unto himself*

Recovered (from the seizure)

I saw Mark Antony offer him a crown—yet 'twas not a
crown neither, 'twas one of these coronets [1]—and,
aside   as I told you, he put it by° once; but, for all that, to   240
gladly / i.e., Antony   my thinking, he would fain° have had it. Then he °
offered it to him again, then he put it by again; but, to
my thinking, he was very loath to lay his fingers off it.
And then he offered it the third time. He put it the
each time   third time by. And, still° as he refused it, the rabble-   245
calloused; rough   ment hooted and clapped their chopped° hands
and threw up their sweaty night-caps and uttered such
a deal of stinking breath because Caesar refused the
crown that it had almost choked Caesar—for he
fainted   swooned° and fell down at it. And for mine own part,   250
dared   I durst ° not laugh for fear of opening my lips and
receiving the bad air.

Cassius

wait   But soft,° I pray you. What, did Caesar swoon?

Casca

He fell down in the marketplace, and foamed at
mouth, and was speechless.   255

Brutus

'Tis very like. He hath the falling sickness. [2]

Cassius

No, Caesar hath it not, but you and I
And honest Casca, we have the falling sickness. [3]

Casca

I know not what you mean by that, but I am sure Caesar
raggedly dressed   fell down. If the tag-rag° people did not clap him and   260
hiss him according as he pleased and displeased them,
are accustomed   as they use° to do the players in the theater, I am no
true man.

Brutus

What said he when he came unto himself? [4]

1　*plucked me ope his doublet*

Opened his jacket (*me* is a mere intensifier modelled on a Latin construction, the ethical dative, calling attention to the speaker)

2　*man of any occupation*

I.e., a working man (like the laborers in 1.1)

3　*he spoke Greek*

And, therefore, could only be understood by the educated citizens

4　*pulling scarves off*

For removing the ceremonial decorations from the statues (see 1.1.63–64)

5　*put to silence*

Removed from office

Casca

Marry, before he fell down, when he perceived the   265
common herd was glad he refused the crown, he
plucked me ope his doublet[1] and offered them his
throat to cut. An° I had been a man of any occupation,[2]

If

his   if I would not have taken him at a° word, I would I
might go to Hell among the rogues. And so he fell.   270
When he came to himself again, he said, if he had done
or said anything amiss, he desired their worships to
think it was his infirmity. Three or four wenches where
I stood cried, "Alas, good soul!" and forgave him with
all their hearts. But there's no heed to be taken of   275
them. If Caesar had stabbed their mothers they would
have done no less.

Brutus

solemnly   And after that he came thus sad° away?

Casca

Aye.

Cassius

Did Cicero say anything?   280

Casca

Aye, he spoke Greek.[3]

Cassius

To what effect?

Casca

if   Nay, an° I tell you that, I'll ne'er look you i' th' face
again. But those that understood him smiled at one
another and shook their heads; but, for mine own   285
part, it was Greek to me. I could tell you more news
too. Murellus and Flavius, for pulling scarves off[4]
Caesar's images, are put to silence.[5] Fare you well. There
was more foolery yet, if I could remember it.

1 *was quick mettle*
   Had a lively intelligence

2 *However he puts on this tardy form*
   However much he affects this
   slow-witted appearance

3 *home to you*
   To your home

4 *the world*
   I.e., the state of affairs

Cassius

Will you sup with me tonight, Casca?   290

Casca

elsewhere No, I am promised forth.°

Cassius

Will you dine with me tomorrow?

Casca

doesn't change Aye, if I be alive and your mind hold°—and your

dinner worth the eating.

Cassius

Good. I will expect you.   295

Casca

Do so. Farewell both.   *He exits.*

Brutus

obtuse What a blunt° fellow is this grown to be!

He was quick mettle[1] when he went to school.

Cassius

So is he now in execution

Of any bold or noble enterprise,   300

However he puts on this tardy form.[2]

seeming ignorance This rudeness° is a sauce to his good wit,

inclination Which gives men stomach° to digest his words

With better appetite.

Brutus

And so it is. For this time I will leave you.   305

Tomorrow, if you please to speak with me,

I will come home to you;[3] or, if you will,

Come home to me, and I will wait for you.

Cassius

I will do so. Till then, think of the world.[4]

                                              Brutus *exits.*

Well, Brutus, thou art noble. Yet I see   310

1   *wrought / From that it is disposed*

    Turned away from its natural inclination (i.e., toward that which is not *honorable*)

2   *their likes*

    Those who think like them

3   *If I were Brutus now and he were Cassius, / He should not humor me.*

    If we were to change places, Brutus would not sway my views (as I have swayed his).

4   *him sure*

    Himself securely

Thy honorable mettle may be wrought

fitting   From that it is disposed. [1] Therefore it is meet°

That noble minds keep ever with their likes, [2]

who is   For who° so firm that cannot be seduced?

ill will   Caesar doth bear me hard,° but he loves Brutus.   315

i.e., Brutus   If I were Brutus now and he° were Cassius,

He should not humor me. [3] I will this night,

handwritings   In several hands,° in at his windows throw,

As if they came from several citizens,

Writings all tending to the great opinion   320

indirectly   That Rome holds of his name, wherein obscurely°

hinted   Caesar's ambition shall be glancèd° at.

And after this let Caesar seat him sure, [4]

For we will shake him or worse days endure.   *He exits.*

1   *Brought you*

    Did you escort

2   *sway*

    **Dominion; Casca's noun however
    anticipates the disruption he
    describes: the shaking Earth does
    sway in a different sense.**

3   *rived the knotty oaks*

    Split the gnarled oaks

4   *exalted with*

    Raised to the height of

5   *tempest dropping fire*

    **A storm with repeated lightning
    bolts**

6   *there is a civil strife in Heaven*

    The gods are at war with one another

7   *Not sensible of fire*

    Unaffected by the flames

8   *drawn / Upon a heap*

    Huddled together

9   *bird of night*

    I.e., the owl

Act 1, Scene 3

Thunder and lightning. Enter **Casca** *and* **Cicero**.

Cicero

evening   Good ev'n,° Casca. Brought you¹ Caesar home?

Why are you breathless? And why stare you so?

Casca

Are not you moved when all the sway² of Earth

unstable   Shakes like a thing unfirm?° Oh, Cicero,

I have seen tempests when the scolding winds   5

Have rived the knotty oaks,³ and I have seen

Th' ambitious ocean swell and rage and foam

To be exalted with⁴ the threat'ning clouds,

But never till tonight, never till now,

Did I go through a tempest dropping fire.⁵   10

Either there is a civil strife in Heaven,⁶

insolent   Or else the world, too saucy° with the gods,

Incenses them to send destruction.

Cicero

astonishing   Why, saw you anything more wonderful?°

Casca

A common slave—you know him well by sight—   15

Held up his left hand, which did flame and burn

Like twenty torches joined, and yet his hand,

Not sensible of fire,⁷ remained unscorched.

have / away   Besides—I ha'° not since put up° my sword—

In front of   Against° the Capitol I met a lion,   20

stared   Who glazed° upon me and went surly by

harming   Without annoying° me; and there were drawn

pale (with fear)   Upon a heap⁸ a hundred ghastly° women,

Transformèd with their fear, who swore they saw

Men all in fire walk up and down the streets.   25

And yesterday the bird of night⁹ did sit

1   *When these prodigies / Do so conjointly meet*

    When these omens occur so close together

2   *"These are their reasons; they are natural"*

    I.e., there is a scientific explanation for the events.

3   *they are portentous things / Unto the climate that they point upon*

    They are ominous incidents, warnings to the region in which they occur. Casca fears that he has witnessed omens portending evil times for Rome.

4   *men may construe things after their fashion, / Clean from the purpose of the things themselves*

    Men may interpret things in their own manner, regardless of the actual meaning of what has been observed.

Even at noon-day upon the marketplace,

Hooting and shrieking. When these prodigies

Do so conjointly meet,[1] let not men say,

"These are their reasons; they are natural,"[2]   30

For I believe they are portentous things

Unto the climate that they point upon.[3]

Cicero

Indeed, it is a strange-disposèd time;

But men may construe things after their fashion,

Completely   Clean° from the purpose of the things themselves.[4]   35

Comes Caesar to the Capitol tomorrow?

Casca

He doth, for he did bid Antonio

Send word to you he would be there tomorrow.

Cicero

Good night then, Casca. This disturbèd sky

Is not to walk in.

Casca

            Farewell, Cicero.   **Cicero** *exits.*   40

Enter **Cassius**.

Cassius

Who's there?

Casca

          A Roman.

Cassius

                    Casca, by your voice.

Casca

Your ear is good. Cassius, what night is this!

Cassius

A very pleasing night to honest men.

1   *Even in the aim*

   **At the exact spot at which it was
   aimed**

2   *from quality and kind*

   Against their natural tendencies

3   *performèd faculties*

   Innate abilties

4   *monstrous state*

   **Unnatural condition (but also the
   Roman *state* under Caesar's
   tyrannous rule)**

Casca

Who ever knew the heavens menace so?

Cassius

Those that have known the Earth so full of faults.   45

For my part, I have walked about the streets,

myself   Submitting me° unto the perilous night

with jacket open   And, thus unbracèd,° Casca, as you see,

thunderbolt   Have bared my bosom to the thunder-stone;°

forked   And when the cross° blue lightning seemed to open   50

The breast of Heaven, I did present myself

Even in the aim¹ and very flash of it.

Casca

why   But wherefore° did you so much tempt the heavens?

It is the part of men to fear and tremble

signs; omens   When the most mighty gods by tokens° send   55

terrify   Such dreadful heralds to astonish° us.

Cassius

stupid   You are dull,° Casca, and those sparks of life

lack   That should be in a Roman you do want,°

use them   Or else you use° not. You look pale, and gaze,

And put on fear, and cast yourself in wonder   60

To see the strange impatience of the heavens;

But if you would consider the true cause

Why all these fires, why all these gliding ghosts,

Why birds and beasts from quality and kind, ²

offer interpretations   Why old men, fools, and children calculate,°   65

ordained forms   Why all these things change from their ordinance°

Their natures and preformèd faculties, ³

unnatural   To monstrous° quality—why, you shall find

That Heaven hath infused them with these spirits

To make them instruments of fear and warning   70

Unto some monstrous state. ⁴

Now could I, Casca, name to thee a man

1 *our fathers' minds are dead*

   **The manly spirit of our ancestors
   no longer lives in us.**

2 *yoke and sufferance*

   Servitude and passivity

3 *I know where I will wear this dagger then: /
   Cassius from bondage will deliver Cassius.*

   **Cassius says that suicide gives him
   the power to escape Caesar's tyranny.**

4 *be retentive to*

   Hold in; imprison

5 *dismiss itself*

   Free itself (through suicide)

6 *know all the world besides*

   Let the rest of the world know

Most like this dreadful night,

That thunders, lightens, opens graves, and roars

As doth the lion in the Capitol—   75

A man no mightier than thyself or me

monstrous In personal action, yet prodigious° grown,

frightening And fearful° as these strange eruptions are.

Casca

'Tis Caesar that you mean. Is it not, Cassius?

Cassius

Let it be who it is. For Romans now   80

sinews Have thews° and limbs like to their ancestors,

But, woe the while, our fathers' minds are dead, [1]

And we are governed with our mothers' spirits.

Our yoke and sufferance [2] show us womanish.

Casca

Indeed, they say the senators tomorrow   85

Mean to establish Caesar as a king,

And he shall wear his crown by sea and land

except In every place save° here in Italy.

Cassius

I know where I will wear this dagger then:

Cassius from bondage will deliver Cassius. [3]   90

i.e., In suicide Therein,° ye gods, you make the weak most strong;

Therein, ye gods, you tyrants do defeat.

Neither Nor° stony tower, nor walls of beaten brass,

Nor airless dungeon, nor strong links of iron

Can be retentive to [4] the strength of spirit.   95

barriers But life, being weary of these worldly bars,°

Never lacks power to dismiss itself. [5]

If I know this, know all the world besides [6]

That part of tyranny that I do bear

I can shake off at pleasure.

continuously   *Thunder still.°*

1   *My answer must be made*

   I must suffer the consequences.

2   *fleering telltale*

   Obsequious tattletale

3   *Hold. My hand.*

   Enough. I offer you my hand.
   (Presumably they shake.)

4   *Be factious*

   Form a faction

5   *Pompey's Porch*

   A portico adjacent to the Roman
   theater built by Pompey in 55 B.C.

Casca

So can I.   100

slave So every bondman° in his own hand bears

The power to cancel his captivity.

Cassius

And why should Caesar be a tyrant then?

Poor man! I know he would not be a wolf

Except for the fact But° that he sees the Romans are but sheep.   105

would be / female deer He were° no lion were not Romans hinds.°

Those that with haste will make a mighty fire

Begin it with weak straws. What trash is Rome,

garbage What rubbish and what offal,° when it serves

As For° the base matter to illuminate   110

So vile a thing as Caesar! But, O grief,

Where hast thou led me? I perhaps speak this

Before a willing bondman; then I know

My answer must be made. [1] But I am armed,

unimportant And dangers are to me indifferent.°   115

Casca

You speak to Casca, and to such a man

That is no fleering telltale. [2] Hold. My hand. [3]

grievances Be factious [4] for redress of all these griefs,°

And I will set this foot of mine as far

whoever As who° goes farthest.

Cassius

There's a bargain made.   120

persuaded Now know you, Casca, I have moved° already

Some certain of the noblest-minded Romans

undertake To undergo° with me an enterprise

Of honorable dangerous consequence;

this time / wait And I do know by this° they stay ° for me   125

In Pompey's Porch. [5] For now, this fearful night,

There is no stir or walking in the streets,

1   *complexion of the element*

   Condition of the sky

2   *I am glad on 't.*

   **I am happy to hear of it (i.e., the
   news that Casca is an ally).**

3   *praetor's chair*

   **Magistrate's seat (i.e., Brutus's
   chair). A *praetor* was a high
   government official just below the
   position of consul.**

And the complexion of the element[1]

appearance is   In favor's° like the work we have in hand:

Most bloody, fiery, and most terrible.   130

Enter **Cinna**.

Casca

out of sight   Stand close° awhile, for here comes one in haste.

Cassius

'Tis Cinna. I do know him by his gait.

He is a friend.—Cinna, where haste you so?

Cinna

To find out you. Who's that? Metellus Cimber?

Cassius

committed   No, it is Casca, one incorporate°   135

waited   To our attempts. Am I not stayed° for, Cinna?

Cinna

I am glad on 't.[2] What a fearful night is this!

There's two or three of us have seen strange sights.

Cassius

Am I not stayed for? Tell me.

Cinna

                 Yes, you are.

O Cassius, if you could   140

But win the noble Brutus to our party—

Cassius

Be you content. Good Cinna, take this paper,

see that   And look° you lay it in the praetor's chair[3]

Where Brutus may but find it; and throw this

In at his window. Set this up with wax   145

Upon old Brutus' statue. All this done,

Go   Repair° to Pompey's Porch, where you shall find us.

Is Decius Brutus and Trebonius there?

1   *yields him ours*

    Joins our side

2   *he sits high in all the people's hearts, /*
    And that which would appear offense in
    us, / His countenance, like richest
    alchemy, / Will change to virtue and to
    worthiness

    Because Brutus is so adored by the
    people, his approval of our
    actions, which might be thought
    dishonorable, will transform them
    into something noble (as alchemy
    changes base metal into gold).

Cinna

All but Metellus Cimber, and he's gone

hurry   To seek you at your house. Well, I will hie,°   150

And so bestow these papers as you bade me.

Cassius

That done, repair to Pompey's Theatre.   **Cinna** *exits.*

Come, Casca, you and I will yet ere day

quarters   See Brutus at his house. Three parts° of him

Is ours already, and the man entire   155

Upon the next encounter yields him ours. [1]

Casca

Oh, he sits high in all the people's hearts,

And that which would appear offense in us,

approved   His countenance,° like richest alchemy,

Will change to virtue and to worthiness. [2]   160

Cassius

Him and his worth and our great need of him

conceived   You have right well conceited.° Let us go,

For it is after midnight, and ere day

We will awake him and be sure of him.   *They exit.*

1 Brutus

This is a key speech in the play,
showing Brutus thinking through
the reasons for assassinating Caesar,
but the soliloquy betrays a circular
reasoning. What should be an act of
reasoning has become a rational-
ization that begins with its conclusion
and then tries to justify it: the
imperative (*must*) is followed by a
series of conditionals (*would, might,
may*). There is, in fact, no evidence in
Brutus's speech—nor in the play—
that Caesar will necessarily become a
tyrant. But if Caesar may not himself
be the tyrant that Brutus fears, anyone
who read Roman history would know
that the death of the Republic led to
the rise of the vicious tyrants—
Tiberius, Caligula, and Nero—whose
rule Brutus, ironically enough, has
helped to bring about.

2 *would be*

Desires to be

3 *that*

The obvious antecedent is *adder*;
i.e., make him into an adder (a
poisonous snake) by giving him
the crown

4 *affections swayed*

I.e., emotions ruled him

Act 2, Scene 1

garden · *Enter **Brutus** in his orchard.*°

Brutus

What, Lucius, ho!

—I cannot by the progress of the stars

i.e., near it is · Give guess how near° to day.—Lucius, I say!

weakness · —I would it were my fault° to sleep so soundly.

—When, Lucius, when? Awake, I say! What, Lucius! 5

*Enter **Lucius**.*

Lucius

Called you, my lord?

Brutus

candle · Get me a taper° in my study, Lucius.

When it is lighted, come and call me here.

Lucius

I will, my lord. *He exits.*

Brutus[1]

i.e., Caesar's · It must be by his° death, and for my part 10

kick · I know no personal cause to spurn° at him

common good · But for the general.° He would be[2] crowned.

How that might change his nature, there's the question.

It is the bright day that brings forth the adder,

demands · And that craves° wary walking. Crown him that,[3] 15

And then I grant we put a sting in him

That at his will he may do danger with.

separates · Th' abuse of greatness is when it disjoins°

Compassion · Remorse° from power. And, to speak truth of Caesar,

I have not known when his affections swayed[4] 20

experience · More than his reason, but 'tis a common proof°

humility · That lowliness° is young ambition's ladder,

91

1   *since the quarrel / Will bear no color for the thing he is*

Since the charge against Caesar cannot be proven by his current behavior

2   *that what he is, augmented, / Would run to these and these extremities*

His nature, with the addition of a crown, would lead him to various kinds of extreme behavior

3   *as his kind*

Like the rest of its species (i.e., serpents)

4   *first*

Most editors emend this Folio reading to *the* "ides," but the appeal to the *calendar* in line 42 suggests that Brutus is uncertain; and he is corrected by Lucius in line 59.

5   *read by them*

The unusual meteor display means that Brutus no longer needs the *taper*, which he had called for in line 7.

Whereto the climber upward turns his face.

rung But when he once attains the upmost round,°

He then unto the ladder turns his back, 25

steps Looks in the clouds, scorning the base degrees°

By which he did ascend. So Caesar may.

Then, lest he may, prevent; and, since the quarrel

Will bear no color for the thing he is, [1]

Fashion it thus: that what he is, augmented, 30

Would run to these and these extremities. [2]

of him And therefore think him° as a serpent's egg,

harmful Which, hatched, would, as his kind,[3] grow mischievous,°

And kill him in the shell.

Enter **Lucius**.

Lucius

study The taper burneth in your closet,° sir. 35

Searching the window for a flint, I found

This paper, thus sealed up, and I am sure

It did not lie there when I went to bed. *(gives him the letter)*

Brutus

Get you to bed again. It is not day.

Is not tomorrow, boy, the first[4] of March? 40

Lucius

I know not, sir.

Brutus

Look in the calendar and bring me word.

Lucius

I will, sir.   *He exits.*

Brutus

meteors The exhalations° whizzing in the air

Give so much light that I may read by them. [5] 45

1   *piece it out*

    Understand it; complete the thought

2   *My ancestors did from the streets of Rome / The Tarquin drive when he was called a king.*

    Brutus's ancestor, Lucius Junius Brutus, expelled Tarquinius Superbus, the last Roman king; see 1.2.160 and note.

3   *Thy full petition*

    All you ask for

4   *whet*

    Sharpen (like a knife)

5   *The genius and the mortal instruments / Are then in council, and the state of a man, / Like to a little kingdom, suffers then / The nature of an insurrection.*

    Brutus draws a conventional parallel between his own internal condition and the external world as he decides whether or not to rise against Caesar. His guardian spirit (*genius*) and his human faculties (*mortal instruments*) debate, dividing his being, as Rome itself will be divided in civil war.

(opens the letter and reads) "Brutus, thou sleep'st. Awake
and see thyself. Shall Rome, etc. Speak, strike,
repair; rectify   redress!"° "Brutus, thou sleep'st. Awake."
Such instigations have been often dropped
Where I have took them up.   50
—"Shall Rome, etc." Thus must I piece it out[1]
"Shall Rome stand under one man's awe?" What Rome?
My ancestors did from the streets of Rome
The Tarquin drive when he was called a king. [2]
"Speak, strike, redress!" Am I entreated   55
a promise   To speak and strike? O Rome, I make thee promise,°
If the redress will follow, thou receivest
from   Thy full petition [3] at° the hand of Brutus!

Enter **Lucius**.

Lucius
Sir, March is wasted fifteen days.   Knock within.
Brutus
'Tis good. Go to the gate. Somebody knocks.   60
                     [**Lucius** exits.]
Since Cassius first did whet [4] me against Caesar,
I have not slept.
Between the acting of a dreadful thing
impulse   And the first motion,° all the interim is
illusion   Like a phantasma° or a hideous dream.   65
guardian spirit   The genius° and the mortal instruments
Are then in council, and the state of a man,
Like to a little kingdom, suffers then
The nature of an insurrection. [5]

Enter **Lucius**.

1   *brother*

    **Brother-in-law. Cassius was
    married to Brutus's sister, Junia.**

2   *if thou path, thy native semblance on*

    **If you follow this course while
    undisguised**

3   *Erebus*

    Dark region of the underworld

Lucius

Sir, 'tis your brother[1] Cassius at the door,　　　　　　　70

Who doth desire to see you.

Brutus

　　　　　　　　　　　Is he alone?

Lucius

No, sir; there are more with him.

Brutus

　　　　　　　　　　　　Do you know them?

Lucius

pulled down　No, sir. Their hats are plucked° about their ears,

And half their faces buried in their cloaks,

identify　That by no means I may discover° them　　　　75

appearance　By any mark of favor.°

Brutus

　　　　　　　　　Let 'em enter.　　[**Lucius** *exits.*]

They are the faction. O conspiracy,

Sham'st thou to show thy dangerous brow by night

on the loose　When evils are most free?° Oh, then by day

Where wilt thou find a cavern dark enough　　　　80

To mask thy monstrous visage? Seek none, conspiracy;

Hide it in smiles and affability.

natural　For if thou path, thy native° semblance on,[2]

Not Erebus[3] itself were dim enough

being thwarted　To hide thee from prevention.°　　　　85

Enter the conspirators: **Cassius, Casca, Decius,**

Cinna, Metellus, *and* **Trebonius**.

Cassius

intruding upon　I think we are too bold upon° your rest.

morning　Good morrow,° Brutus. Do we trouble you?

1   *But honors*
    Feels anything but respect for

2   *watchful cares*
    Concerns that keep you awake

Brutus

I have been up this hour, awake all night.

Know I these men that come along with you?

Cassius

Yes, every man of them, and no man here   90

But honors[1] you, and every one doth wish

You had but that opinion of yourself

Which every noble Roman bears of you.

This is Trebonius.

Brutus

                    He is welcome hither.

Cassius

This, Decius Brutus.

Brutus

                    He is welcome too.   95

Cassius

This, Casca. This, Cinna, and this, Metellus Cimber.

Brutus

They are all welcome.

What watchful cares[2] do interpose themselves

Betwixt your eyes and night?

Cassius

Shall I entreat a word?   [**Brutus** *and* **Cassius**] *whisper.*   100

Decius

Here lies the east; doth not the day break here?

Casca

No.

Cinna

Oh, pardon, sir, it doth, and yon gray lines

interlace   That fret° the clouds are messengers of day.

Casca

mistaken   You shall confess that you are both deceived.°   105

1 *face of men*

(Sad) expressions of the people

2 *by lottery*

By chance (probably referring to the Roman practice of selecting by lot a tenth of the soldiers to die as punishment for rebellion)

3 *And what other oath / Than honesty to honesty engaged*

And what other oath (do we need) besides the exchange of our pledges of honor

4 *cautelous*

Cautious; wary; crafty

5 *carrions*

I.e., old people on the brink of death (literally, corpses)

Here, as I point my sword, the sun arises,

advancing   Which is a great way growing° on the south,

Considering   Weighing° the youthful season of the year.

Some two months hence, up higher toward the north

i.e., The sun / due   He° first presents his fire, and the high° east   110

as does   Stands, as° the Capitol, directly here.

Brutus

i.e., of you   Give me your hands all over,° one by one.

Cassius

And let us swear our resolution.

Brutus

No, not an oath. If not the face of men,[1]

suffering   The sufferance° of our souls, the time's abuse—   115

at once   If these be motives weak, break off betimes,°

empty   And every man hence to his idle° bed.

arrogant   So let high-sighted° tyranny range on

i.e., these motives   Till each man drop by lottery.[2] But if these,°

As I am sure they do, bear fire enough   120

strengthen   To kindle cowards and to steel° with valor

The melting spirits of women, then, countrymen,

What need we any spur but our own cause

motivate   To prick° us to redress? What other bond

discreet   Than secret° Romans that have spoke the word   125

equivocate   And will not palter?° And what other oath

Than honesty to honesty engaged,[3]

because of   That this shall be or we will fall for° it?

Leave the swearing to   Swear° priests and cowards and men cautelous,[4]

passive   Old feeble carrions,[5] and such suffering° souls   130

oppression   That welcome wrongs;° unto bad causes swear

that   Such creatures as° men doubt. But do not stain

straightforward   The even° virtue of our enterprise,

indomitable   Nor th' insuppressive° mettle of our spirits,

1 *guilty of a several bastardy*

I.e., unworthy of its Roman lineage

2 *sound him*

Find out what he thinks

3 *no whit*

Not at all

4 *break with him*

Reveal our plans to him

either   To think that or° our cause or our performance   135
require   Did need° an oath, when every drop of blood
            That every Roman bears—and nobly bears—
            Is guilty of a several bastardy [1]
            If he do break the smallest particle
            Of any promise that hath passed from him.   140

Cassius

But what of Cicero? Shall we sound him? [2]
I think he will stand very strong with us.

Casca

Let us not leave him out.

Cinna

                    No, by no means.

Metellus

            Oh, let us have him, for his silver hairs
reputation   Will purchase us a good opinion°   145
            And buy men's voices to commend our deeds.
            It shall be said his judgment ruled our hands;
            Our youths and wildness shall no whit [3] appear
dignity   But all be buried in his gravity.°

Brutus

Oh, name him not. Let us not break with him, [4]   150
For he will never follow anything
That other men begin.

Cassius

                    Then leave him out.

Casca

Indeed he is not fit.

Decius

Shall no man else be touched, but only Caesar?

Cassius

fitting   Decius, well urged. I think it is not meet°   155
            Mark Antony, so well beloved of Caesar,

1   *of him*
     Him to be

2   *shrewd contriver*
     Clever strategist

3   *come by*
     Get at

4   *And let our hearts, as subtle masters do, /
     Stir up their servants to an art of rage /
     And after seem to chide 'em*

     **The lines seem to urge hypocrisy
     and until the twentieth century
     were usually cut in performance.**

5   *Our course will seem too bloody, Caius
     Cassius, / To cut the head off and then hack
     the limbs. . . . For he can do no more than
     Caesar's arm / When Caesar's head is off.*

     **Brutus's speech is yet another
     example of his naïveté and
     inability to apply his own
     undoubted virtue to practical
     situations. Brutus argues that the
     death of Caesar will appear as a
     noble sacrifice by killing him
     publicly and everyone taking
     responsibility for the act. His idea
     that this will legitimize, even
     sanctify, the reality of the killing is
     exposed as a mad idea in the
     course of the play. Brutus's goal is
     to kill *Caesar's spirit*, but the irony is
     that only Caesar's body is killed; his
     spirit lives on, literally as his ghost**
     appears in Act Four, scene two, but
     also in the presence of Octavius (as
     well as in the recurrence of tyranny
     in human history). Brutus's naïveté
     is also evident in his misjudgment
     about killing Antony. His high-
     mindedness keeps him from seeing
     the world as it is.

Should outlive Caesar. We shall find of him[1]

resources   A shrewd contriver,[2] and you know his means,°

capitalizes on   If he improve° them, may well stretch so far

harm   As to annoy° us all—which to prevent,   160

Let Antony and Caesar fall together.

Brutus

Our course will seem too bloody, Caius Cassius,

To cut the head off and then hack the limbs,

malice   Like wrath in death and envy° afterwards—

For Antony is but a limb of Caesar.   165

Let's be sacrificers but not butchers, Caius.

We all stand up against the spirit of Caesar,

And in the spirit of men there is no blood.

Oh, that we then could come by[3] Caesar's spirit

And not dismember Caesar! But, alas,   170

noble   Caesar must bleed for it, and, gentle° friends,

Let's kill him boldly but not wrathfully.

Let's carve him as a dish fit for the gods,

Not hew him as a carcass fit for hounds,

And let our hearts, as subtle masters do,   175

i.e., hands   Stir up their servants° to an act of rage

rebuke   And after seem to chide° 'em.[4] This shall make

malicious   Our purpose necessary and not envious,°

Which so appearing to the common eyes,

We shall be called purgers, not murderers.   180

as for   And for° Mark Antony, think not of him,

For he can do no more than Caesar's arm

When Caesar's head is off.[5]

Cassius

                        Yet I fear him,

deep-rooted   For in the engrafted° love he bears to Caesar—

Brutus

Alas, good Cassius, do not think of him.   185

1   *take thought*

    Become melancholy

2   *And that were much he should*

    But it is more than one can expect
    that he would go so far.

3   *clock*

    A famous anachronism, as there
    could have been no striking clock in
    44 B.C., but another example of the
    play's concern with the mechanics
    and measurement of time. This
    striking of the clock recalls the
    spectacular striking of the clock at
    the end of Marlowe's *Dr. Faustus* when
    his time runs out and the devils
    come to seize his soul and drag him
    to Hell, a noted event on the early
    modern stage.

4   *Quite from the main*

    Completely in contrast to the
    essential

5   *apparent prodigies*

    Visible omens (see 1.3.15–32)

6   *augurers*

    Religious seers who interpret omens

7   *unicorns may be betrayed with trees*

    According to legend, one could
    capture a unicorn by provoking the
    animal and then retreating behind
    a tree; when the unicorn charged,
    its horn would impale the tree and,
    thus stuck, the animal could be
    easily captured.

8   *men with flatterers*

    Men can be snared by flattery (as
    easily as animals are by traps).

If he love Caesar, all that he can do
Is to himself: take thought[1] and die for Caesar.
And that were much he should,[2] for he is given
To sports, to wildness, and much company.
Trebonius

danger   There is no fear° in him. Let him not die,   190
For he will live and laugh at this hereafter.   *Clock strikes.*
Brutus
Peace! Count the clock.[3]
Cassius

                The clock hath stricken three.

Trebonius
'Tis time to part.
Cassius

           But it is doubtful yet
Whether Caesar will come forth today or no,
For he is superstitious grown of late,   195
Quite from the main[4] opinion he held once

portents; divinations   Of fantasy, of dreams, and ceremonies.°
It may be these apparent prodigies,[5]
The unaccustomed terror of this night,
And the persuasion of his augurers[6]   200
May hold him from the Capitol today.
Decius
Never fear that. If he be so resolved,

persuade   I can o'ersway° him, for he loves to hear
That unicorns may be betrayed with trees,[7]

mirrors / pits   And bears with glasses,° elephants with holes,°   205

nets   Lions with toils,° and men with flatterers.[8]
But when I tell him he hates flatterers,
He says he does, being then most flatterèd.
Let me work.

1 *give his humor the true bent*

   **Manipulate his mood in the right
   way**

2 *doth bear Caesar hard*

   Has ill will toward Caesar

3 *fashion him*

   Bring him around to our side

4 *put on*

   Show; reveal

5 *formal constancy*

   **Artistic control (i.e., by always
   staying in character)**

For I can give his humor the true bent, [1]   210
And I will bring him to the Capitol.
Cassius
escort Nay, we will all of us be there to fetch° him.
Brutus
latest By the eighth hour. Is that the uttermost?°
Cinna
Be that the uttermost, and fail not then.
Metellus
Caius Ligarius doth bear Caesar hard, [2]   215
rebuked Who rated° him for speaking well of Pompey.
I wonder none of you have thought of him.
Brutus
to Now, good Metellus, go along by° him.
He loves me well, and I have given him reasons.
Send him but hither, and I'll fashion him. [3]   220
Cassius
us The morning comes upon 's.° We'll leave you, Brutus.
—And, friends, disperse yourselves. But all remember
What you have said, and show yourselves true Romans.
Brutus
Good gentlemen, look fresh and merrily.
Let not our looks put on [4] our purposes,   225
But bear it, as our Roman actors do,
unwavering With untired° spirits and formal constancy. [5]
And so good morrow to you every one.
                [The conspirators] exit. **Brutus** *remains.*
—Boy! Lucius!—Fast asleep? It is no matter.
Enjoy the honey-heavy dew of slumber.   230
premonitions Thou hast no figures° nor no fantasies,
anxiety Which busy care° draws in the brains of men.
Therefore thou sleep'st so sound.

1   *across*

    Folded (denoting sadness or worry)

2   *an effect of humor*

    The result of a temporary mood

3   *know you Brutus*

    Recognize you as Brutus

Enter **Portia**.

Portia

         Brutus, my lord.

Brutus

Portia, what mean you? Wherefore rise you now?

good for / expose   It is not for° your health thus to commit°   235

Your weak condition to the raw, cold morning.

Portia

discourteously   Nor for yours neither. Y' have ungently,° Brutus,

Stole from my bed. And yesternight, at supper,

You suddenly arose and walked about,

Musing and sighing, with your arms across, [1]   240

And when I asked you what the matter was,

You stared upon me with ungentle looks.

I urged you further, then you scratched your head

And too impatiently stamped with your foot.

Still   Yet° I insisted; yet you answered not,   245

wave   But with an angry wafture° of your hand

Gave sign for me to leave you. So I did,

Fearing to strengthen that impatience

also   Which seemed too much enkindled, and withal°

Hoping it was but an effect of humor, [2]   250

its   Which sometime hath his° hour with every man.

It will not let you eat, nor talk, nor sleep,

And could it work so much upon your shape

disposition   As it hath much prevailed on your condition,°

I should not know you Brutus. [3] Dear my lord,   255

Make me acquainted with your cause of grief.

Brutus

I am not well in health, and that is all.

1   *come by it*

    Restore his health

2   *unbracèd*

    With his jacket open

3   *rheumy and unpurgèd*

    Damp and not yet purified by
    sunlight

4   *Is it excepted*

    Is there a stipulation that

5   *in sort or limitation*

    Only in some manner, or within
    certain boundaries

Portia

Brutus is wise, and were he not in health,
He would embrace the means to come by it. [1]

Brutus

Why, so I do. Good Portia, go to bed.   260

Portia

healthy Is Brutus sick? And is it physical°
damp air To walk unbracèd [2] and suck up the humors°
          Of the dank morning? What, is Brutus sick,
          And will he steal out of his wholesome bed
          To dare the vile contagion of the night   265
          And tempt the rheumy and unpurgèd [3] air
          To add unto his sickness? No, my Brutus.
malady You have some sick offense° within your mind,
          Which by the right and virtue of my place
          I ought to know of; [*kneeling*] and upon my knees   270
entreat I charm° you, by my once-commended beauty,
i.e., marriage vow By all your vows of love, and that great vow°
          Which did incorporate and make us one,
          That you unfold to me, your self, your half,
downcast Why you are heavy° and what men tonight   275
access Have had resort° to you. For here have been
          Some six or seven who did hide their faces
          Even from darkness.

Brutus

                              Kneel not, gentle Portia.

Portia

i.e., need to [*rising*] I should not need,° if you were gentle Brutus.
          Within the bond of marriage, tell me, Brutus,   280
          Is it excepted [4] I should know no secrets
          That appertain to you? Am I your self
          But, as it were, in sort or limitation, [5]
stay To keep° with you at meals, comfort your bed,

1   *suburbs*

Outskirts (the *suburbs* of Shakepeare's London, less regulated than the city, were notorious for various forms of unruly activity, including brothels, hence *harlot* in line 287)

2   *Cato's daughter*

Portia's reference to her father identifies her as a key figure within the genealogy of the intellectual life of the Roman Republic. See LONGER NOTE, page 284.

3   *I have made strong proof of my constancy, / Giving myself a voluntary wound / Here in the thigh.*

Plutarch describes how Portia observed and was troubled by her husband's distress but knew that she could not rightfully question him until she had proven herself a worthy confidant. To demonstrate her strength and self-control, Portia took "a little razor such as barbers occupy to pare men's nails" and gave herself "a great gash withal in her thigh, that she was straight all of a gore-blood." She then showed this wound to Brutus, claiming that "now I have found by experience that no pain nor grief whatsoever can overcome me," thus entreating him to disclose his secrets.

4   *charactery*

Writing (i.e., what is written on or meant by the furrows in Brutus's *sad brows*)

And talk to you sometimes? Dwell I but in the suburbs [1]   285
Of your good pleasure? If it be no more,
Portia is Brutus' harlot, not his wife.

Brutus

You are my true and honorable wife,
As dear to me as are the ruddy drops
That visit my sad heart.   290

Portia

If this were true, then should I know this secret.
nevertheless   I grant I am a woman, but withal°
A woman that Lord Brutus took to wife.
I grant I am a woman, but withal
A woman well-reputed, Cato's daughter. [2]   295
Think you I am no stronger than my sex,
Being so fathered and so husbanded?
secrets   Tell me your counsels.° I will not disclose 'em.
fortitude   I have made strong proof of my constancy,°
Giving myself a voluntary wound   300
Here in the thigh. [3] Can I bear that with patience,
And not my husband's secrets?

Brutus
                              O ye gods,
Render me worthy of this noble wife!   *Knock [within].*
Hark, hark! One knocks. Portia, go in awhile,
And by and by thy bosom shall partake   305
The secrets of my heart.
explain   All my engagements I will construe° to thee,
worried   All the charactery [4] of my sad° brows.
Leave me with haste.   **Portia** *exits.*

Enter **Lucius** *and* **Ligarius**.

1   *how?*

Could either be "how are you" or
an exclamation of surprise at his
presence

2   *wear a kerchief*

Wrapping a *kerchief* or shawl
around the head was a customary
practice for the sick in Shakespeare's time.

Lucius, who's that knocks?

Lucius

Here is a sick man that would speak with you. *310*

Brutus

Caius Ligarius, that Metellus spake of.

—Boy, stand aside.—Caius Ligarius, how?[1]

Ligarius

Please accept Vouchsafe° "good morrow" from a feeble tongue.

Brutus

Oh, what a time have you chose out, brave Caius,

To wear a kerchief![2] Would you were not sick! *315*

Ligarius

I am not sick if Brutus have in hand

Any exploit worthy the name of honor.

Brutus

Such an exploit have I in hand, Ligarius,

Had you a healthful ear to hear of it.

Ligarius

[*removes his scarf*] By all the gods that Romans bow

before, *320*

I here discard my sickness! Soul of Rome,

Worthy Brave° son derived from honorable loins,

Thou, like an exorcist, hast conjured up

deadened My mortifièd° spirit. Now bid me run,

And I will strive with things impossible, *325*

Yea, get the better of them. What's to do?

Brutus

healthy A piece of work that will make sick men whole.°

Ligarius

But are not some whole that we must make sick?

Brutus

That must we also. What it is, my Caius,

I shall unfold to thee as we are going *330*

To whom it must be done.

Ligarius

Proceed   Set° on your foot,
And with a heart new-fired I follow you
To do I know not what, but it sufficeth
That Brutus leads me on.   *Thunder.*

Brutus

                                        Follow me, then.   *They exit.*

1 *stood on ceremonies*
   Heeded portents

2 *watch*
   **Night watchmen (common in
   Shakespeare's London, not in
   Caesar's Rome)**

Act 2, Scene 2

dressing gown   *Thunder and lightning. Enter Julius* **Caesar** *in his nightgown.*°

Caesar

Neither   Nor° Heaven nor Earth have been at peace tonight.

Thrice hath Calphurnia in her sleep cried out,

"Help, ho! They murder Caesar!"—Who's within?

Enter a **Servant**.

Servant

My lord.

Caesar

immediate   Go bid the priests do present° sacrifice   5

what will happen   And bring me their opinions of success.°

Servant

I will, my lord.   *He exits.*

Enter **Calphurnia**.

Calphurnia

What mean you, Caesar? Think you to walk forth?

You shall not stir out of your house today.

Caesar

Caesar shall forth. The things that threatened me   10

Ne'er looked but on my back. When they shall see

The face of Caesar, they are vanishèd.

Calphurnia

Caesar, I never stood on ceremonies, [1]

someone   Yet now they fright me. There is one° within,

Besides the things that we have heard and seen,   15

Recounts most horrid sights seen by the watch. [2]

given birth   A lioness hath whelpèd° in the streets,

1   *right form*

Standard combat order

opened   And graves have yawned° and yielded up their dead.
                 Fierce fiery warriors fight upon the clouds
                 In ranks and squadrons and right form¹ of war,   20
                 Which drizzled blood upon the Capitol.
                 The noise of battle hurtled in the air.
                 Horses do neigh, and dying men did groan,
                 And ghosts did shriek and squeal about the streets.
normal experience O Caesar! These things are beyond all use,°   25
                 And I do fear them.

Caesar
                                    What can be avoided
determined   Whose end is purposed° by the mighty gods?
Nonetheless   Yet° Caesar shall go forth, for these predictions
Are as applicable Are° to the world in general as to Caesar.

Calphurnia
                 When beggars die there are no comets seen.   30
proclaim   The heavens themselves blaze° forth the death of
                     princes.

Caesar
                 Cowards die many times before their deaths;
                 The valiant never taste of death but once.
                 Of all the wonders that I yet have heard,
                 It seems to me most strange that men should fear,   35
                 Seeing that death, a necessary end,
                 Will come when it will come.

                     Enter a **Servant**.

                                    What say the augurers?

Servant
                 They would not have you to stir forth today.
sacrificed animal Plucking the entrails of an offering° forth,
                 They could not find a heart within the beast.   40

1 *in shame of cowardice*

   To shame cowards

2 *Caesar should be a beast without a heart*

   Caesar would lack courage
   (through an obvious reference to
   the augury in lines 39–40)

Caesar

The gods do this in shame of cowardice. [1]
Caesar should be a beast without a heart [2]
If he should stay at home today for fear.
No, Caesar shall not. Danger knows full well
That Caesar is more dangerous than he.   45
We are two lions littered in one day,
And I the elder and more terrible.
And Caesar shall go forth.

Calphurnia

                                    Alas, my lord,
i.e., overconfidence   Your wisdom is consumed in confidence.°
Do not go forth today. Call it my fear   50
That keeps you in the house, and not your own.
We'll send Mark Antony to the senate house,
And he shall say you are not well today.
[*kneels*] Let me, upon my knee, prevail in this.

Caesar

Mark Antony shall say I am not well,   55
mood   And for thy humor° I will stay at home.

                                    [**Calphurnia** *rises.*]

Enter **Decius**.

Here's Decius Brutus. He shall tell them so.

Decius

morning   Caesar, all hail! Good morrow,° worthy Caesar.
I come to fetch you to the senate house.

Caesar

opportune   And you are come in very happy° time   60
To bear my greeting to the senators
And tell them that I will not come today.

1   *She dreamt tonight she saw my statue, /*
     Which, like a fountain with an hundred
     spouts, / Did run pure blood; and many
     lusty Romans / Came smiling and did
     bathe their hands in it.

     **Calphurnia's dream is recorded in
     Shakespeare's major source,
     Plutarch's *Lives*, but there she
     dreams of a fallen tower as a
     symbol of her husband's death.
     Shakespeare changes this to a
     statue and adds the detail about
     the hundred spouts of blood in
     which the smiling Romans wash
     their hands, clearly to make
     Calphurnia's fears anticipate the
     events that follow. Caesar is quick
     to dismiss his wife's dreams as
     meaningless, obviously confident
     in his own ability to control
     whatever fate can throw at him.
     The relationship between Caesar
     and Calphurnia, like that of Brutus
     and Portia, suggests that if men
     listened more closely to women
     they might avoid some of the
     dangers they inflict on themselves
     through their own stubborn pride.**

2   *apply for*

     Interpret as

3   *men shall press / For tinctures, stains,*
     relics, and cognizance

     **Men shall crowd around (*press*)
     trying to get remembrances of
     Caesar's greatness (*tinctures* and
     stains are handkerchiefs dipped in
     some martyr's blood; *relics* are
     bones or objects that belonged to
     some holy person; *cognizance* is a
     heraldic emblem identifying
     members of a noble household).**

"Cannot" is false, and that I dare not, falser.
I will not come today. Tell them so, Decius.
Calphurnia
Say he is sick.
Caesar
                Shall Caesar send a lie? 65
Have I in conquest stretched mine arm so far
To be afeard to tell graybeards the truth?
Decius, go tell them Caesar will not come.
Decius
Most mighty Caesar, let me know some cause,
Lest I be laughed at when I tell them so. 70
Caesar
The cause is in my will: I will not come.
That is enough to satisfy the senate.
But for your private satisfaction,
Because I love you, I will let you know.

keeps   Calphurnia here, my wife, stays° me at home. 75
last night   She dreamt tonight° she saw my statue,
Which, like a fountain with an hundred spouts,
stalwart   Did run pure blood; and many lusty° Romans
Came smiling and did bathe their hands in it. [1]
i.e., these images   And these° does she apply for[2] warnings and portents 80
And evils imminent, and on her knee
Hath begged that I will stay at home today.
Decius
This dream is all amiss interpreted.
It was a vision fair and fortunate.
Your statue spouting blood in many pipes, 85
In which so many smiling Romans bathed,
Signifies that from you great Rome shall suck
Reviving blood, and that great men shall press
For tinctures, stains, relics, and cognizance. [3]

1   *it were a mock / Apt to be rendered for*
    someone to say
    Some sarcastic remark is likely to
    be made, such as

2   *reason to my love is liable*
    Discretion is outweighed by my
    love (for you)

This by Calphurnia's dream is signified.   90

Caesar

And this way have you well expounded it.

Decius

I have, when you have heard what I can say.

And know it now: the senate have concluded

To give this day a crown to mighty Caesar.

If you shall send them word you will not come,   95

Their minds may change. Besides, it were a mock

Apt to be rendered for someone to say, [1]

"Break up the senate till another time

When Caesar's wife shall meet with better dreams."

If Caesar hide himself, shall they not whisper,   100

"Lo, Caesar is afraid"?

Pardon me, Caesar. For my dear, dear love

advancement   To your proceeding° bids me tell you this,

And reason to my love is liable. [2]

Caesar

How foolish do your fears seem now, Calphurnia!   105

I am ashamèd I did yield to them.

Give me my robe, for I will go.

> *Enter* **Brutus, Ligarius, Metellus, Casca,**
> **Trebonius, Cinna,** *and* **Publius**.

And look where Publius is come to fetch me.

Publius

Good morrow, Caesar.

Caesar

                            Welcome, Publius.

—What, Brutus, are you stirred so early too?   110

—Good morrow, Casca.—Caius Ligarius,

Caesar was ne'er so much your enemy

1   *ague*

   (Pronounced Ay-gyoo) fever

2   *prepare within*

   I.e., put out wine in the other room

3   *I am to blame to be thus waited for.*

   Caesar apologizes for his lack of
   hospitality in not having immediately provided wine for his guests.

4   *every "like" is not the same*

   There is a difference between really
   being friends and merely being *like
   friends* (line 127).

As that same ague [1] which hath made you lean.
—What is 't o'clock?
Brutus

                Caesar, 'tis strucken eight.

Caesar
I thank you for your pains and courtesy.   115

        Enter **Antony**.

See, Antony, that revels long a-nights,
Is, notwithstanding, up. Good morrow, Antony.
Antony
So to most noble Caesar.
Caesar

             [to servant] Bid them prepare within. [2]
I am to blame to be thus waited for. [3]   **[Servant** *exits.*]
—Now, Cinna.—Now, Metellus.—What, Trebonius,   120
I have an hour's talk in store for you.
Remember that you call on me today.
Be near me that I may remember you.
Trebonius
Caesar, I will. *[aside]* And so near will I be
That your best friends shall wish I had been further.   125
Caesar
Good friends, go in and taste some wine with me.
And we, like friends, will straightway go together.
Brutus
[aside] That every "like" is not the same, [4] O Caesar,
grieves The heart of Brutus earns° to think upon.   *They exit.*

1   **Artemidorus**

     **Artemidorus, according to
     Plutarch, was a teacher of rhetoric
     and "very familiar with certain of
     Brutus's confederates."**

2   *Security gives way to conspiracy.*

     **Overconfidence provides
     opportunity for betrayal.**

3   *Out of the teeth of emulation*

     Safe from the danger of envy

Act 2, Scene 3

Enter **Artemidorus**, [1] [*with a letter*].

Artemidorus

[*reads*] "Caesar, beware of Brutus. Take heed of Cassius.
Come not near Casca. Have an eye to Cinna. Trust not
Trebonius. Mark well Metellus Cimber. Decius Brutus
loves thee not. Thou hast wronged Caius Ligarius.

directed   There is but one mind in all these men, and it is bent°   5
against Caesar. If thou be'st not immortal, look
about you. Security gives way to conspiracy.[2] The

friend   mighty gods defend thee! Thy lover,° Artemidorus."
Here will I stand till Caesar pass along,

petitioner   And as a suitor° will I give him this.   10
My heart laments that virtue cannot live
Out of the teeth of emulation.[3]
If thou read this, O Caesar, thou mayest live;

conspire   If not, the fates with traitors do contrive.°   *He exits.*

1　*take good note*

Observe carefully

2　*bustling rumor*

Commotion; agitated noise

Act 2, Scene 4

*Enter **Portia** and **Lucius**.*

Portia

I prithee, boy, run to the senate house.
Stay not to answer me but get thee gone.
Why dost thou stay?

Lucius

                To know my errand, madam.

Portia

I would have had thee there and here again
Ere I can tell thee what thou shouldst do there.   5
fortitude [*aside*] O constancy,° be strong upon my side;
Set a huge mountain 'tween my heart and tongue!
I have a man's mind but a woman's might.
secrets How hard it is for women to keep counsel!°
still —Art thou here yet? °

Lucius

                Madam, what should I do?   10
Run to the Capitol and nothing else?
And so return to you and nothing else?

Portia

Yes. Bring me word, boy, if thy lord look well,
For he went sickly forth. And take good note[1]
petitioners What Caesar doth, what suitors° press to him.   15
Hark, boy! What noise is that?

Lucius

I hear none, madam.

Portia

Prithee, listen well.
fight I heard a bustling rumor[2] like a fray,°
And the wind brings it from the Capitol.   20

Lucius

In truth   Sooth,° madam, I hear nothing.

Enter the **Soothsayer**.

Portia

Come hither, fellow. Which way hast thou been?

Soothsayer

At mine own house, good lady.

Portia

What is 't o'clock?

Soothsayer

About the ninth hour, lady.   25

Portia

Is Caesar yet gone to the Capitol?

Soothsayer

Madam, not yet. I go to take my stand

To see him pass on to the Capitol.

Portia

Thou hast some suit to Caesar, hast thou not?

Soothsayer

That I have, lady. If it will please Caesar   30

To be so good to Caesar as to hear me,

I shall beseech him to befriend himself.

Portia

Why? Know'st thou any harm's intended towards him?

Soothsayer

occur   None that I know will be; much that I fear may chance.°

Good morrow to you. Here the street is narrow;   35

The throng that follows Caesar at the heels,

magistrates   Of senators, of praetors,° common suitors,

Will crowd a feeble man almost to death.

1   *in*

    I.e., back into the house

2   *Brutus hath a suit / That Caesar will not grant.*

    Portia offers Lucius a plausible motive for Brutus being at the Capitol, perhaps fearing that he has overheard her word *enterprise* (line 43) and guessed at the conspiracy.

empty   I'll get me to a place more void° and there

Speak to great Caesar as he comes along.   *He exits.* 40

Portia

I must go in. [1] [*aside*] Aye me, how weak a thing

The heart of woman is! O Brutus,

The heavens speed thee in thine enterprise!

Surely   Sure° the boy heard me. [*to* **Lucius**] Brutus hath a suit

That Caesar will not grant. [2]—Oh, I grow faint.   45

—Run, Lucius, and commend me to my lord.

Say I am merry. Come to me again

And bring me word what he doth say to thee.

                 They exit [*separately*].

1   *schedule*

   Paper (i.e., the letter from 2.3
   warning Caesar of the conspiracy)

2   *Sirrah*

   Term of address, often
   contemptuous, generally used for
   persons of lower social rank

3   *give place*

   Get out of the way.

Act 3, Scene 1

Flourish. Enter **Caesar**, **Brutus**, **Cassius**, **Casca**, **Decius**,
Metellus, **Trebonius**, **Cinna**, **Antony**, **Lepidus**,
Publius, [*and* **Popilius** *Lena, with a crowd of people,*
including] **Artemidorus** *and the* **Soothsayer**.

Caesar

[*to the* **Soothsayer**] The ides of March are come.

Soothsayer

Aye, Caesar, but not gone.

Artemidorus

[*offering his letter*] Hail, Caesar! Read this schedule.[1]

Decius

[*offering* **Caesar** *another paper*] Trebonius doth desire you
    to o'er-read

At your best leisure this his humble suit.   5

Artemidorus

O Caesar, read mine first, for mine's a suit

That touches° Caesar nearer. Read it, great Caesar.   *concerns*

Caesar

What touches us ourself shall be last served.°   *considered*

Artemidorus

Delay not, Caesar. Read it instantly.

Caesar

What, is the fellow mad?

Publius

            [*to* **Artemidorus**] Sirrah,[2] give place.[3] 10

Cassius

[*to* **Artemidorus**] What, urge you your petitions in the
    street?

Come to the Capitol.

            [*Caesar's party moves away.* **Caesar** *sits.*]

1   *Cassius or Caesar never shall turn back*

Either Cassius or Caesar will not return alive.

2   *presently prefer his suit*

Immediately put forth his petition

Popilius

[*to* **Cassius**] I wish your enterprise today may thrive.

Cassius

What enterprise, Popilius?

Popilius

          Fare you well. [*approaches* **Caesar**]

Brutus

[*to* **Cassius**] What said Popilius Lena?   15

Cassius

He wished today our enterprise might thrive.

I fear our purpose is discoverèd.

Brutus

proceeds   Look how he makes° to Caesar. Mark him.

Cassius

quick   Casca, be sudden,° for we fear prevention

    —Brutus, what shall be done? If this be known,   20

Cassius or Caesar never shall turn back, [1]

For I will slay myself.

Brutus

             Cassius, be constant.

Popilius Lena speaks not of our purposes.

i.e., change expression   For, look, he smiles, and Caesar doth not change.°

Cassius

Trebonius knows his time, for, look you, Brutus,   25

He draws Mark Antony out of the way.

          [**Trebonius** *and* **Antony** *exit.*]

Decius

Where is Metellus Cimber? Let him go

And presently prefer his suit [2] to Caesar.

Brutus

ready   He is addressed.° Press near and second him.

1   *couchings and these lowly courtesies*

   Kneelings and deep bows

2   *turn preordinance and first decree / Into*
   the law of children

   Make immutable laws and first
   principles seem merely arbitrary
   rules in some children's game

3   *To think that Caesar bears such rebel*
   blood / That will be thawed from the true
   quality / With that which melteth fools

   To think that Caesar's passion is so
   uncontrolled that it will allow his
   essential excellence to be
   compromised by any of those
   tricks that melt fools' hearts

4   *Low-crookèd*

   Disingenuous; dishonest; also
   indicating the angle of the body
   bent in a bow

5   *satisfied*

   I.e., persuaded to do something he
   had not initially intended

6   *freedom of repeal*

   Permission to return to Rome from
   exile

Cinna

will raise   Casca, you are the first that rears° your hand.   30

Caesar

Are we all ready? What is now amiss

That Caesar and his senate must redress?

Metellus

powerful   [*kneeling*] Most high, most mighty, and most puissant°

    Caesar,

Metellus Cimber throws before thy seat

An humble heart—

Caesar

stop   I must prevent° thee, Cimber.   35

These couchings and these lowly courtesies [1]

passion   Might fire the blood° of ordinary men

And turn preordinance and first decree

so foolish   Into the law of children. [2] Be not fond°

To think that Caesar bears such rebel blood   40

As   That° will be thawed from the true quality

With that which melteth fools [3]—I mean, sweet words,

obsequious   Low-crookèd [4] curtsies, and base spaniel° fawning.

Thy brother by decree is banishèd.

If thou dost bend and pray and fawn for him,   45

kick/dog   I spurn° thee like a cur° out of my way.

You should know   Know° Caesar doth not wrong, nor without cause

Will he be satisfied. [5]

Metellus

Is there no voice more worthy than my own

To sound more sweetly in great Caesar's ear   50

recall from exile   For the repealing° of my banished brother?

Brutus

[*kneeling*] I kiss thy hand, but not in flattery, Caesar,

Desiring thee that Publius Cimber may

Have an immediate freedom of repeal. [6]

1   *could pray to move*

    Were capable of begging others to change their minds

2   *holds on his rank*

    Maintains his position

3   *Wilt thou lift up Olympus?*

    Do the impossible (and lift Mount *Olympus*). Caesar also likens himself to a god, since Mount Olympus was the home of the classical gods.

4   *Doth not Brutus bootless kneel?*

    I.e., since even Brutus (whom I love dearly) pleads in vain, why do you try?

5   *Speak, hands, for me!*

    Let my actions speak for me!

Caesar

What, Brutus?

Cassius

           [*kneeling*] Pardon, Caesar; Caesar, pardon.   55

As low as to thy foot doth Cassius fall

restitution of citizenship   To beg enfranchisement° for Publius Cimber.

Caesar

I could be well moved if I were as you.

If I could pray to move, [1] prayers would move me.

i.e., immovable   But I am constant° as the Northern Star,   60

Of whose true-fixed and resting quality

equal   There is no fellow° in the firmament.

innumerable   The skies are painted with unnumbered° sparks;

They are all fire, and every one doth shine,

But there's but one in all doth hold his place.   65

So in the world: 'tis furnished well with men,

perceptive   And men are flesh and blood and apprehensive;°

Yet in the number I do know but one

That unassailable holds on his rank, [2]

Unshaked of motion—and that I am he,   70

Let me a little show it even in this:

That I was constant Cimber should be banished

And constant do remain to keep him so.

Cinna

[*kneeling*] O Caesar—

Caesar

           Hence! Wilt thou lift up Olympus? [3]

Decius

[*kneeling*] Great Caesar—

Caesar

to no avail   Doth not Brutus bootless° kneel? [4]   75

Casca

Speak, hands, for me! [5]

1   *Et tu, Brutè?*

    "And you, Brutus?" (Latin).
    Caesar's surprise at Brutus's
    betrayal is the most famous line in
    Julius Caesar, derived from the Greek
    words recorded in Suetonius's
    (c. A.D. 70 –160) account of Caesar's
    death in *The Twelve Caesars*.
    Suetonius has Caesar say to Brutus,
    "You too, my child?", probably a
    reference to the common belief
    that Brutus was Caesar's biological
    son. The line first appears in *The
    True Tragedie of Richard Duke of Yorke*
    (better known now as *Henry VI, Part
    Three*), which was published in
    1595. It is spoken by King Edward as
    the Duke of Clarence changes sides
    to fight for the Lancastrian faction,
    showing how easy early modern
    writers found it to make
    connections between English and
    Roman history.

2   *common pulpits*

    Public platforms used for speeches

3   *Ambition's debt*

    I.e., what Caesar's ambition is
    owed

4   *confounded with this mutiny*

    Amazed by this confusion (what
    surprises Publius is not the
    murder, as he is one of the
    conspirators, but the tumult that
    follows)

5   *Talk not of standing*

    Brutus rejects Metellus's idea that
    they must *Stand fast together* (line
    87), since he is confident that the
    people will understand and accept
    the explanation for the assass-
    ination. Cassius, as usual, knows
    better; see lines 92–93.

6   *your age some mischief*

    Some harm to your aged body

They stab **Caesar**, [*in turn,* **Casca** *first,* **Brutus** *last*].

Caesar

Et tu, Brutè? [1]—Then fall, Caesar.   *Dies.*

Cinna

Liberty! Freedom! Tyranny is dead!

Run hence, proclaim, cry it about the streets.

Cassius

go to Some to° the common pulpits [2] and cry out,   80

"Liberty, freedom, and enfranchisement!"

[*Noise and confusion. Some plebeians and senators exit.*]

Brutus

People and senators, be not affrighted.

Fly not. Stand still. Ambition's debt [3] is paid.

Casca

Go to the pulpit, Brutus.

Decius

                         And Cassius too.

Brutus

Where's Publius?   85

Cinna

Here, quite confounded with this mutiny. [4]

Metellus

Stand fast together, lest some friend of Caesar's

Should chance—

Brutus

Talk not of standing. [5]—Publius, good cheer.

There is no harm intended to your person,   90

Nor to no Roman else. So tell them, Publius.

Cassius

And leave us, Publius, lest that the people,

Rushing on us, should do your age some mischief. [6]

1   *abide*

    Suffer the consequences for

2   *'tis but the time / And drawing days out*
    that men stand upon

    It is only the exact moment of
    death and how to extend their lives
    that men care about.

3   *Peace, freedom, and liberty*

    These lines are, of course, deeply
    ironic. The desire for freedom and
    liberty was a cornerstone of
    republican political programs; but
    the fact that conspirators bathed in
    blood from an assassination
    proclaim such words shows just
    how far Rome has degenerated
    from its republican ideals and how
    blind they are to what they have
    done.

Brutus

Do so. And let no man abide¹ this deed
But we the doers.   95

[**Publius** *exits with all but the other conspirators.*]

Enter **Trebonius**.

Cassius

Where is Antony?
Trebonius

in fear   Fled to his house amazed.°

Men, wives, and children stare, cry out, and run
As if   As° it were doomsday.
Brutus

                              Fates, we will know your pleasures.

That we shall die, we know; 'tis but the time
And drawing days out that men stand upon. ²   *100*
Cassius

Why, he that cuts off twenty years of life
Cuts off so many years of fearing death.
Brutus

Grant that, and then is death a benefit.
So are we Caesar's friends that have abridged
His time of fearing death. Stoop, Romans, stoop,   *105*
And let us bathe our hands in Caesar's blood
Up to the elbows and besmear our swords.
i.e., the Forum   Then walk we forth, even to the marketplace,°
And, waving our red weapons o'er our heads,
Let's all cry, "Peace, freedom, and liberty!" ³   *110*
Cassius

Stoop, then, and wash.
[*They kneel, smearing their hands and swords with* **Caesar**'s *blood.*]
                              How many ages hence

1   *Pompey's basis*

    The base of Pompey's statue

2   *knot*

    Group (i.e., the conspirators)

3   *feared*

    **Antony must mean this as "felt
    dread and reverance for" as is
    appropriate to a ruler, but the word
    is well chosen to suggest a
    seeming sympathy with the
    conspirators.**

4   *be resolved*

    Receive a satisfactory explanation

Shall this our lofty scene be acted over

languages   In states unborn and accents° yet unknown!

Brutus

plays   How many times shall Caesar bleed in sport,°

stretched out   That now on Pompey's basis[1] lies along°   115

No worthier than the dust!

Cassius

So oft as that shall be,

So often shall the knot[2] of us be called

The men that gave their country liberty.

Decius

What, shall we forth?

Cassius

                Aye, every man away.   120

honor   Brutus shall lead, and we will grace° his heels

With the most boldest and best hearts of Rome.

Enter **Servant**.

Brutus

Quiet!   Soft!° Who comes here? A friend of Antony's.

Servant

[*kneeling*] Thus, Brutus, did my master bid me kneel.

[*falls prostrate*] Thus did Mark Antony bid me fall down,   125

And, being prostrate, thus he bade me say:

honorable   "Brutus is noble, wise, valiant, and honest.°

Caesar was mighty, bold, royal, and loving.

Say I love Brutus, and I honor him.

Say I feared[3] Caesar, honored him, and loved him.   130

allow it   If Brutus will vouchsafe° that Antony

May safely come to him and be resolved[4]

How Caesar hath deserved to lie in death,

Mark Antony shall not love Caesar dead

1   *untrod state*

     **Unprecedented state of affairs (but
     also inevitably heard as, the newly
     established Roman state)**

2   *so please him come*

     If it pleases him to come

3   *well to friend*

     As a friend

4   *my misgiving still / Falls shrewdly to the
     purpose*

     **My apprehensions are always right
     on the mark.**

5   *Who else must be let blood? Who else
     is rank?*

     **"Who else must be bled [i.e., killed]?
     Who else is swollen and diseased?"
     Bloodletting was a common medical
     procedure that used leeches or
     incisions to draw out blood and
     purge the patient of infection.**

So well as Brutus living, but will follow   135
The fortunes and affairs of noble Brutus
Through Thorough° the hazards of this untrod state[1]
With all true faith." So says my master Antony.

Brutus
Thy master is a wise and valiant Roman;
I never thought him worse.   140
Tell him, so please him come[2] unto this place,
He shall be satisfied and, by my honor,
Depart untouched.

Servant
immediately   [*rising*] I'll fetch him presently.°

                                        Servant *exits.*

Brutus
I know that we shall have him well to friend.[3]

Cassius
I wish we may. But yet have I a mind   145
always That fears him much, and my misgiving still°
Falls shrewdly to the purpose.[4]

        Enter **Antony**.

Brutus
But here comes Antony.—Welcome, Mark Antony.

Antony
O mighty Caesar! Dost thou lie so low?
Are all thy conquests, glories, triumphs, spoils,   150
Shrunk to this little measure? Fare thee well.
—I know not, gentlemen, what you intend,
Who else must be let blood? Who else is rank?[5]
fitting If I myself, there is no hour so fit°
As Caesar's death's hour, nor no instrument   155
Of half that worth as those your swords made rich

1   *purpled hands do reek and smoke*

    **Bloodied hands steam (from
    Caesar's freshly shed blood); both
    reek and *smoke* mean "give off
    steam"**

2   *so pity pity*

    **I.e., pity for Rome outweighed their
    (the conspirators') pity for Caesar**

3   *Our arms in strength of malice and our
    hearts / Of brothers' temper do receive
    you in*

    **I.e., our arms, though strong in
    their opposition (to Caesar), and
    our hearts, full of brotherly love,
    welcome you**

4   *the disposing of new dignities*

    **Giving out positions in the new
    government**

With the most noble blood of all this world.

ill will   I do beseech ye, if you bear me hard,°

Now, whilst your purpled hands do reek and smoke,[1]

If I live   Fulfill your pleasure. Live° a thousand years,   160

ready   I shall not find myself so apt° to die.

manner   No place will please me so, no mean° of death,

As here by Caesar and by you cut off,

most excellent   The choice° and master spirits of this age.

Brutus

O Antony, beg not your death of us.   165

Though now we must appear bloody and cruel—

As by our hands and this our present act

only   You see we do—yet see you but° our hands

And this the bleeding business they have done.

full of pity   Our hearts you see not. They are pitiful;°   170

for   And pity to° the general wrong of Rome—

As fire drives out fire, so pity pity[2]—

Hath done this deed on Caesar. For your part,

blunted   To you our swords have leaden° points, Mark Antony.

Our arms in strength of malice and our hearts   175

Of brothers' temper do receive you in[3]

With all kind love, good thoughts, and reverence.

Cassius

Your voice shall be as strong as any man's

In the disposing of new dignities.[4]

Brutus

Only be patient till we have appeased   180

The multitude, beside themselves with fear,

reveal to   And then we will deliver° you the cause

Why I, that did love Caesar when I struck him,

Have thus proceeded.

Antony

                     I doubt not of your wisdom.

1   *bayed*

Brought to bay ; cornered; a
hunting term meaning
"surrounded by hounds" (i.e., the
conspirators)

2   *hart*

Stag; also a pun on *heart*

3   *Signed in thy spoil*

Marked with the evidence of your
slaughter

4   *crimsoned in thy Lethe*

Covered in your life blood; *Lethe*
(pronounced with two syllables) is
the river in Hades , whose waters
induced forgetfulness in the dead
as they entered the underworld.

Let each man render me his bloody hand. 185
First, Marcus Brutus, will I shake with you.
—Next, Caius Cassius, do I take your hand.
—Now, Decius Brutus, yours. —Now yours, Metellus.
—Yours, Cinna. —And, my valiant Casca, yours.
—Though last, not least in love, yours, good Trebonius. 190
Gentlemen all, alas, what shall I say?

credibility My credit° now stands on such slippery ground
imagine; regard That one of two bad ways you must conceit° me:
Either a coward or a flatterer.
That I did love thee, Caesar, —Oh, 'tis true. 195
If then thy spirit look upon us now,
more deeply Shall it not grieve thee dearer° than thy death
To see thy Antony making his peace,
Shaking the bloody fingers of thy foes—
Most noble!—in the presence of thy corpse? 200
Had I as many eyes as thou hast wounds,
Weeping as fast as they stream forth thy blood,
join It would become me better than to close°
In terms of friendship with thine enemies.
Pardon me, Julius! Here wast thou bayed,[1] brave hart;[2] 205
Here didst thou fall; and here thy hunters stand,
Signed in thy spoil[3] and crimsoned in thy Lethe.[4]
O world, thou wast the forest to this hart,
And this indeed, O world, the heart of thee.
How like a deer, strucken by many princes, 210
Dost thou here lie!

Cassius

Mark Antony—

Antony

Pardon me, Caius Cassius.
Even the The° enemies of Caesar shall say this;

1 *cold modesty*

Emotionless moderation

2 *Or else were this*

Otherwise this would be

Then, in a friend, it is cold modesty. [1]   215

Cassius

I blame you not for praising Caesar so.

agreement But what compact° mean you to have with us?

marked down; counted Will you be pricked° in number of our friends,

proceed Or shall we on° and not depend on you?

Antony

Therefore I took your hands, but was indeed   220

Swayed from the point by looking down on Caesar.

Friends am I with you all and love you all

Upon this hope: that you shall give me reasons

in what way Why and wherein° Caesar was dangerous.

Brutus

Or else were this [2] a savage spectacle!   225

considerations Our reasons are so full of good regard°

That were you, Antony, the son of Caesar,

You should be satisfied.

Antony

                That's all I seek,

a petitioner And am, moreover suitor° that I may

Bring forth / Forum Produce° his body to the marketplace,°   230

And in the pulpit, as becomes a friend,

ceremony Speak in the order° of his funeral.

Brutus

You shall, Mark Antony.

Cassius

                Brutus, a word with you.

[*aside to* **Brutus**] You know not what you do. Do not

    consent

That Antony speak in his funeral.   235

Know you how much the people may be moved

By that which he will utter?

1   *tide of times*

Course of history

Brutus

[*aside to* **Cassius**] By your pardon,

i.e., will go   I will° myself into the pulpit first

And show the reason of our Caesar's death.

proclaim   What Antony shall speak, I will protest°   240

He speaks by leave and by permission,

And that we are contented Caesar shall

proper   Have all true° rites and lawful ceremonies.

benefit us   It shall advantage° more than do us wrong.

Cassius

happen   [*aside to* **Brutus**] I know not what may fall.° I like it not.   245

Brutus

Mark Antony, here, take you Caesar's body.

You shall not in your funeral speech blame us,

But speak all good you can devise of Caesar,

And say you do 't by our permission,

Otherwise   Else ° shall you not have any hand at all   250

About his funeral; and you shall speak

In the same pulpit whereto I am going,

After my speech is ended.

Antony

Be it so.

I do desire no more.

Brutus

Prepare the body then and follow us.   255

They all exit, but **Antony** *remains.*

Antony

Oh, pardon me, thou bleeding piece of earth,

That I am meek and gentle with these butchers!

Thou art the ruins of the noblest man

That ever livèd in the tide of times. [1]

Woe to the hand that shed this costly blood!   260

Over thy wounds now do I prophesy

1 *with custom of fell deeds*

By the repeated experience of savage (*fell*) actions

2 *ranging*

Roaming, as an animal hunts for prey

3 *Ate*

(pronounced AH-tay) Greek goddess of discord and destruction

4 *"Havoc!"*

Military order to destroy without mercy

5 *Octavius Caesar*

Julius Caesar's great-nephew, adopted son and heir; later known as Augustus Caesar

mute	(Which, like dumb° mouths, do ope their ruby lips
	To beg the voice and utterance of my tongue)
	A curse shall light upon the limbs of men.
National	Domestic° fury and fierce civil strife	265
overwhelm	Shall cumber° all the parts of Italy.
	Blood and destruction shall be so in use,
	And dreadful objects so familiar,
	That mothers shall but smile when they behold
cut in pieces	Their infants quartered° with the hands of war,	270
	All pity choked with custom of fell deeds;[1]
	And Caesar's spirit, ranging[2] for revenge,
	With Ate[3] by his side come hot from Hell,
regions	Shall in these confines° with a monarch's voice
loose	Cry "Havoc!"[4] and let slip° the dogs of war,	275
	That this foul deed shall smell above the earth
i.e., dying	With carrion° men groaning for burial.

Enter Octavius's **Servant**.

You serve Octavius Caesar,[5] do you not?
Servant
I do, Mark Antony.
Antony
Caesar did write for him to come to Rome. 280
Servant
He did receive his letters and is coming,
And bid me say to you by word of mouth—
[*seeing* **Caesar**'s *body*] O Caesar!
Antony

swollen (with grief)	Thy heart is big.° Get thee apart and weep.
Sorrow	Passion,° I see, is catching, for mine eyes,	285
i.e., tears	Seeing those beads° of sorrow stand in thine,
	Began to water. Is thy master coming?

1   *seven leagues*

About twenty-one miles; a league
is a unit of length approximately
three miles

2   *Rome*

Punning on "room"; both words
were pronounced similarly (see
1.2.157)

3   *young Octavius*

Octavius was twenty-one. Plutarch
says that Antony undervalued him
"because he was very young."

4   *Lend me your hand.*

Antony asks for help carrying
Caesar's body off stage.

Servant

camps; lodges   He lies° tonight within seven leagues¹ of Rome.

Antony

Ride / happened   Post° back with speed and tell him what hath chanced.°

Here is a mourning Rome, a dangerous Rome,   290

No Rome² of safety for Octavius yet.

Hurry   Hie° hence and tell him so. Yet stay awhile.

return   Thou shalt not back° till I have borne this corpse

test   Into the marketplace. There shall I try,°

react to   In my oration, how the people take°   295

action   The cruel issue° of these bloody men,

According to the which, thou shalt discourse

To young Octavius³ of the state of things.

Lend me your hand.⁴   *They exit [with **Caesar**'s body].*

1   *be satisfied*

    Get a satisfactory explanation

2   *give me audience*

    Listen to me

3   *part the numbers*

    Divide the crowd

4   *public reasons*

    I.e., reasons given publicly (or
    possibly "reasons concerning the
    public good")

5   *have respect to*

    Keep in mind

Act 3, Scene 2

Enter **Brutus** *and* **Cassius** *with the* **Plebeians**.

Plebeians
We will be satisfied! ¹ Let us be satisfied!

Brutus
Then follow me and give me audience, ² friends.
—Cassius, go you into the other street
And part the numbers. ³
—Those that will hear me speak, let 'em stay here;   5
Those that will follow Cassius, go with him,
And public reasons ⁴ shall be renderèd
Of Caesar's death.

First Plebeian
                              I will hear Brutus speak.

Second Plebeian
I will hear Cassius and compare their reasons
separately   When severally° we hear them renderèd.   10

> [**Cassius** *exits, followed by some* **Plebeians**.]
> [**Brutus**] *goes into the pulpit.*

Third Plebeian
The noble Brutus is ascended. Silence!

Brutus
end (of my speech)   Be patient till the last.°
friends   Romans, countrymen, and lovers!° Hear me for my
cause and be silent that you may hear. Believe me for
mine honor and have respect to ⁵ mine honor that you   15
Judge   may believe. Censure° me in your wisdom and awake
reason   your senses° that you may the better judge. If there be
any in this assembly, any dear friend of Caesar's, to him
I say that Brutus' love to Caesar was no less than his.
If then that friend demand why Brutus rose against   20
Caesar, this is my answer: not that I loved Caesar less,

1   *you shall do to Brutus*

    I.e., you will do to me (if I act as Caesar did)

2   *The question of his death is enrolled*

    The reasons for his death are recorded

3   *a place in the commonwealth*

    I.e., the full rights of a Roman citizen

but that I loved Rome more. Had you rather Caesar
were living and die all slaves than that Caesar were dead
to live all free men? As Caesar loved me, I weep for him.
As he was fortunate, I rejoice at it. As he was valiant, I   25
honor him. But, as he was ambitious, I slew him. There
is tears for his love, joy for his fortune, honor for his
valor, and death for his ambition. Who is here so base
slave   that would be a bondman?° If any, speak—for him
uncivilized; ignorant   have I offended. Who is here so rude° that would not be   30
a Roman? If any, speak—for him have I offended. Who
worthless   is here so vile° that will not love his country? If any,
speak—for him have I offended. I pause for a reply.

All

None, Brutus, none!

Brutus

Then none have I offended. I have done no more to   35
i.e., Caesar's   Caesar than you shall do to Brutus. [1] The question of his°
diminished   death is enrolled [2] in the Capitol. His glory not extenuated°
magnified   wherein he was worthy, nor his offenses enforced° for
which he suffered death.

*Enter Mark **Antony** [and others] with **Caesar**'s body.*

Here comes his body, mourned by Mark Antony, who,   40
though he had no hand in his death, shall receive the
benefit of his dying—a place in the commonwealth, [3]
as which of you shall not? With this I depart: that, as I
friend   slew my best lover° for the good of Rome, I have the
same dagger for myself when it shall please my country   45
to need my death.   [*descends from the pulpit*]

All

Live, Brutus! Live, live!

1   *Do grace*

    Show respect

2   *grace his speech*

    **Courteously listen to Antony's
    speech**

First Plebeian

Bring him with triumph home unto his house!

Second Plebeian

Give him a statue with his ancestors!

Third Plebeian

Let him be Caesar!

Fourth Plebeian

Caesar's better parts   50

Shall be crowned in Brutus!

First Plebeian

We'll bring him to his house with shouts and clamors.

Brutus

My countrymen—

Second Plebeian

Peace! Silence! Brutus speaks.

First Plebeian

Peace, ho!

Brutus

Good countrymen, let me depart alone,   55

And, for my sake, stay here with Antony.

Do grace¹ to Caesar's corpse and grace his speech²

Relating   Tending° to Caesar's glories, which Mark Antony

By our permission is allowed to make.

I do entreat you not a man depart,   60

Save I alone, till Antony have spoke.   *He exits.*

First Plebeian

Stay ho, and let us hear Mark Antony.

Third Plebeian

pulpit   Let him go up into the public chair.°

We'll hear him. Noble Antony, go up.

Antony

beholden; indebted   For Brutus' sake, I am beholding° to you.   65

[ascends the pulpit]

1 **Antony**

Antony's funeral oration for Caesar is an expansion of the bare details provided by Plutarch, who notes that Antony mingled "his oration with lamentable words," and so moved the listeners "unto pity and compassion" for the dead Caesar. When Antony showed the people the "bloody garments of the dead, thrust through in many places with their swords," he put "the people into such a fury" that they burned Caesar's body in the marketplace and then ran "to the murderers' houses to set them afire, and to make them come out and to fight."

2 *under leave of*

With permission from

Fourth Plebeian

What does he say of Brutus?

Third Plebeian

He says for Brutus' sake

He finds himself beholding to us all.

Fourth Plebeian

'Twere best he speak no harm of Brutus here.

First Plebeian

This Caesar was a tyrant.

Third Plebeian

Nay, that's certain.

We are blest that Rome is rid of him.   70

Fourth Plebeian

Peace! Let us hear what Antony can say.

Antony

You gentle Romans—

All

Peace, ho! Let us hear him.

Antony [1]

Friends, Romans, countrymen, lend me your ears.

I come to bury Caesar, not to praise him.

The evil that men do lives after them;   75

buried   The good is oft interrèd° with their bones.

So let it be with Caesar. The noble Brutus

Hath told you Caesar was ambitious.

If it were so, it was a grievous fault,

paid the penalty for   And grievously hath Caesar answered° it.   80

Here, under leave of [2] Brutus and the rest

(For Brutus is an honorable man;

So are they all, all honorable men),

Come I to speak in Caesar's funeral.

i.e., Caesar   He° was my friend, faithful and just to me,   85

But Brutus says he was ambitious,

1   *general coffers*

    State treasury

2   *the Lupercal*

    Feast of Lupercal; see 1.1.66 and note

3   *I thrice presented him a kingly crown, /*
    Which he did thrice refuse

    **The offering of the crown to Caesar
    and his refusal of it (see 1.2.222–250)
    could be seen as a sign of Caesar's
    loyalty to the ideals of the Republic
    and his distaste for the trappings of
    monarchy. (Romans were suspicious
    of monarchy ever since the exile of
    the Tarquins, the final kings of
    Rome, which was precipitated by the
    rape of the Roman matron Lucrece
    by Tarquinus Sextus, son of
    Tarquinus Superbus. That event,
    which was narrated in Shakespeare's
    long poem *The Rape of Lucrece*,
    published in 1594, eventually led to
    the foundation of the Republic.) But
    it might also be a sign that Caesar
    knew that he already possessed real
    power and would only weaken his
    position by being seen to subvert the
    ideals of the Republic. Whichever
    way we view the evidence, it is clear
    that Shakespeare shows that the
    Republic is on its last legs and that its
    institutions can no longer function
    to protect or strengthen it.**

4   *brutish*

    **Unintelligent, but punning
    sardonically on *Brutus***

And Brutus is an honorable man.

i.e., Caesar   He° hath brought many captives home to Rome

Whose ransoms did the general coffers[1] fill.

Did this in Caesar seem ambitious?   90

When that the poor have cried, Caesar hath wept.

Ambition should be made of sterner stuff.

Yet Brutus says he was ambitious,

And Brutus is an honorable man.

You all did see that on the Lupercal[2]   95

I thrice presented him a kingly crown,

Which he did thrice refuse.[3] Was this ambition?

Yet Brutus says he was ambitious,

And sure he is an honorable man.

I speak not to disprove what Brutus spoke,   100

But here I am to speak what I do know.

You all did love him once, not without cause.

prevents   What cause withholds° you then to mourn for him?

O judgment, thou are fled to brutish[4] beasts,

And men have lost their reason. Bear with me.   105

My heart is in the coffin there with Caesar,

And I must pause till it come back to me.   [*He weeps.*]

First Plebeian

Methinks there is much reason in his sayings.

Second Plebeian

If thou consider rightly of the matter,

Caesar has had great wrong.

Third Plebeian

                                    Has he, masters?   110

I fear there will a worse come in his place.

Fourth Plebeian

Marked ye his words? He would not take the crown,

Therefore 'tis certain he was not ambitious.

1   *dear abide it*

    Greatly suffer for it

2   *none so poor to do him reverence*

    **I.e., even the poorest man is now
    greater than Caesar and needs not pay
    him homage.**

3   *napkins in his sacred blood*

    **Handkerchiefs dipped in Caesar's
    blood; the reference, like that to
    beg a hair of him for memory (line 134),
    is to the keeping of sacred relics,
    physical objects associated with a
    martyr that became objects of
    reverence (see 2.2.88–89 and
    note).**

First Plebeian

If it be found so, some will dear abide it. [1]

Second Plebeian

Poor soul! His eyes are red as fire with weeping.   115

Third Plebeian

There's not a nobler man in Rome than Antony.

Fourth Plebeian

pay attention to   Now mark° him. He begins again to speak.

Antony

Only   But° yesterday the word of Caesar might

Have stood against the world. Now lies he there,

And none so poor to do him reverence. [2]   120

incite   O masters, if I were disposed to stir°

Your hearts and minds to mutiny and rage,

I should do Brutus wrong and Cassius wrong,

Who, you all know, are honorable men.

I will not do them wrong. I rather choose   125

To wrong the dead, to wrong myself and you,

Than I will wrong such honorable men.

But here's a parchment with the seal of Caesar.

study   I found it in his closet.° 'Tis his will.

common people   Let but the commons° hear this testament—   130

Which, pardon me, I do not mean to read—

And they would go and kiss dead Caesar's wounds

And dip their napkins in his sacred blood, [3]

Yea, beg a hair of him for memory,

And, dying, mention it within their wills,   135

Bequeathing it as a rich legacy

children   Unto their issue.°

Fourth Plebeian

We'll hear the will. Read it, Mark Antony!

All

The will, the will! We will hear Caesar's will.

1   *o'ershot myself*

Said more than I meant to

Antony

Have patience, gentle friends. I must not read it.   140

fitting   It is not meet° you know how Caesar loved you.

You are not wood, you are not stones, but men,

And, being men, hearing the will of Caesar,

It will inflame you; it will make you mad.

'Tis good you know not that you are his heirs,   145

For, if you should—Oh, what would come of it!

Fourth Plebeian

Read the will! We'll hear it, Antony!

must   You shall° read us the will, Caesar's will.

Antony

Will you be patient? Will you stay awhile?

I have o'ershot myself¹ to tell you of it.   150

I fear I wrong the honorable men

Whose daggers have stabbed Caesar. I do fear it.

Fourth Plebeian

They were traitors! "Honorable men"?

All

The will! The testament!

Second Plebeian

They were villains, murderers! The will! Read the will!   155

Antony

You will compel me, then, to read the will?

Then make a ring about the corpse of Caesar,

And let me show you him that made the will.

permission   Shall I descend? And will you give me leave?°

All

Come down.

Second Plebeian

       Descend.

Third Plebeian

         You shall have leave.

1   *Nervii*

Germanic tribe conquered by Caesar
in 57 B.C.

2   *unkindly*

Cruelly (but also "unnaturally"); the
same doubleness of meaning
operates in *unkindest* in line 180.

[**Antony** *descends from the pulpit.*]

Fourth Plebeian

                        A ring!   160

Stand round.

First Plebeian

away from / bier   Stand from° the hearse.° Stand from the body.

Second Plebeian

Make room   Room° for Antony, most noble Antony!

Antony

farther   Nay, press not so upon me. Stand far° off.

All

Move   Stand back. Room! Bear° back.   165

Antony

   If you have tears, prepare to shed them now.

cloak   You all do know this mantle.° I remember

   The first time ever Caesar put it on.

   'Twas on a summer's evening in his tent,

   That day he overcame the Nervii. [1]   [*shows the cloak*]   170

   Look, in this place ran Cassius' dagger through.

gash / malicious   See what a rent° the envious° Casca made.

   Through this the well-belovèd Brutus stabbed,

   And, as he plucked his cursèd steel away,

   Mark how the blood of Caesar followed it,   175

   As rushing out of doors to be resolved

   If Brutus so unkindly [2] knocked or no.

i.e., favorite   For Brutus, as you know, was Caesar's angel.°

   Judge, O you gods, how dearly Caesar loved him!

   This was the most unkindest cut of all,   180

   For when the noble Caesar saw him stab,

   Ingratitude, more strong than traitors' arms,

Completely   Quite° vanquished him. Then burst his mighty heart,

cloak   And, in his mantle° muffling up his face,

   Even at the base of Pompey's statue,   185

1   *what weep you when you but behold /*
    Our Caesar's vesture wounded?
    How will you weep when you see
    Caesar's torn clothing?

Which all the while ran blood, great Caesar fell.
Oh, what a fall was there, my countrymen!
Then I, and you, and all of us fell down,
Whilst bloody treason flourished over us.
Oh, now you weep, and I perceive you feel 190
force The dint° of pity. These are gracious drops.
Kind souls, what weep you when you but behold
Our Caesar's vesture wounded?[1] Look you here,
[*lifts the cloth covering* **Caesar**'s body]
by Here is himself, marred, as you see, with° traitors.
First Plebeian
O piteous spectacle! 195
Second Plebeian
O noble Caesar!
Third Plebeian
O woeful day!
Fourth Plebeian
O traitors, villains!
First Plebeian
O most bloody sight!
Second Plebeian
We will be revenged. 200
All
Get to work Revenge! About!° Seek! Burn! Fire! Kill! Slay!
Let not a traitor live!
Antony
Wait Stay,° countrymen!
First Plebeian
Peace there! Hear the noble Antony.
Second Plebeian
We'll hear him. We'll follow him. We'll die with him! 205
Antony
Good friends, sweet friends, let me not stir you up

1   *private griefs*

Personal grievances

2   *public leave*

Permission to speak in public

3   *right on*

Directly

4   *were I Brutus, / And Brutus Antony, there were an Antony / Would ruffle up your spirits*

I.e., if I had the skill for oratory that Brutus has, I would be an orator who could stir up your anger.

5   *put a tongue / In every wound of Caesar*

Make each of Caesar's wounds cry out for revenge

To such a sudden flood of mutiny.
They that have done this deed are honorable.
What private griefs[1] they have, alas, I know not,
That made them do it. They are wise and honorable,   210
And will, no doubt, with reasons answer you.
I come not, friends, to steal away your hearts.
I am no orator, as Brutus is,
But, as you know me all, a plain blunt man
That love my friend, and that they know full well   215
That gave me public leave[2] to speak of him.
For I have neither wit, nor words, nor worth,
Action, nor utterance, nor the power of speech
To stir men's blood. I only speak right on.[3]
I tell you that which you yourselves do know,   220
Show you sweet Caesar's wounds, poor poor dumb
    mouths,
And bid them speak for me. But were I Brutus,
And Brutus Antony, there were an Antony
Would ruffle up your spirits[4] and put a tongue
In every wound of Caesar[5] that should move   225
The stones of Rome to rise and mutiny.

All

We'll mutiny!

First Plebeian

                    We'll burn the house of Brutus!

Third Plebeian

Away then; come! Seek the conspirators!

Antony

Yet hear me, countrymen; yet hear me speak.

All

Peace, ho! Hear Antony, most noble Antony!   230

Antony

Why, friends, you go to do you know not what.

1   *seventy-five drachmas*

    **A drachma was a silver coin, and
    the gift was, as Plutarch says, "a
    liberal legacy."**

2   *common pleasures*

    Public parks

3   *We'll burn his body in the holy place, / And
    with the brands fire the traitors' houses.*

    **We'll make a funeral pyre by the
    temple and use the burning wood
    (*brands*) to set fire to the traitors'
    homes.**

4   *Pluck down*

    Tear loose

For what   Wherein° hath Caesar thus deserved your loves?

Alas, you know not. I must tell you then.

You have forgot the will I told you of.

All

Most true. The will! Let's stay and hear the will!   235

Antony

Here is the will, and, under Caesar's seal,

To every Roman citizen he gives—

individual   To every several° man—seventy-five drachmas. [1]

Second Plebeian

Most noble Caesar! We'll revenge his death!

Third Plebeian

O royal Caesar!   240

Antony

Hear me with patience.

All

Peace, ho!

Antony

promenades   Moreover, he hath left you all his walks,°

gardens   His private arbors, and new-planted orchards,°

On this side Tiber. He hath left them you,   245

And to your heirs forever, common pleasures [2]

To walk abroad and recreate yourselves.

Here was a Caesar! When comes such another?

First Plebeian

Never, never.—Come, away, away!

We'll burn his body in the holy place,   250

And with the brands fire the traitors' houses. [3]

Take up the body.

Second Plebeian

Go fetch fire.

Third Plebeian

Pluck down[4] benches.

1   *thither will I straight*

    I will go there immediately.

2   *upon a wish*

    At exactly the right moment

3   *Are rid*

    Have ridden

4   *Belike they had some notice of the people /*
    How I had moved them.

    I.e., probably they heard how I
    roused the people (against them)

Fourth Plebeian

window frames / shutters Pluck down forms,° windows,° anything.   255

> **Plebeians** *exit* [*with* **Caesar**'*s body*].

Antony

Discord Now let it work. Mischief,° thou art afoot.

Take thou what course thou wilt!

> *Enter* **Servant**.

> How now, fellow?

Servant

Sir, Octavius is already come to Rome.

Antony

Where is he?

Servant

He and Lepidus are at Caesar's house.   260

Antony

And thither will I straight[1] to visit him.

He comes upon a wish.[2] Fortune is merry

And in this mood will give us anything.

Servant

I heard him say Brutus and Cassius

Are rid[3] like madmen through the gates of Rome.   265

Antony

Belike they had some notice of the people

How I had moved them.[4] Bring me to Octavius.

> *They exit.*

1 *unluckily charge my fantasy*

Ominously weigh on my imagination

2 *you were best*

You had better (do so)

3 *bear me a bang*

Take a punch from me

Act 3, Scene 3

*Enter **Cinna the Poet**, and after him the **Plebeians**.*

Cinna the Poet

last night   I dreamt tonight° that I did feast with Caesar,

And things unluckily charge my fantasy.[1]

out   I have no will to wander forth° of doors,

Yet something leads me forth.

First Plebeian

What is your name?   5

Second Plebeian

Whither are you going?

Third Plebeian

Where do you dwell?

Fourth Plebeian

Are you a married man or a bachelor?

Second Plebeian

honestly   Answer every man directly.°

First Plebeian

Aye, and briefly.   10

Fourth Plebeian

Aye, and wisely.

Third Plebeian

Aye, and truly, you were best.[2]

Cinna the Poet

What is my name? Whither am I going? Where do I
dwell? Am I a married man or a bachelor? Then, to
answer every man directly and briefly, wisely and   15
truly—wisely I say, I am a bachelor.

Second Plebeian

That's as much as to say they are fools that marry. You'll
bear me a bang[3] for that, I fear. Proceed, directly.

1   *Directly*

Cinna the Poet playfully jokes, with
Directly meaning (1) honestly (as has
been demanded in line 9) and (2)
immediately. His innocent wordplay
indicates how badly he has misun-
derstood the situation he is in.

2   *turn him going*

Send him on his way (to his death)

3   exit, [carrying **Cinna the Poet**]

An incident based closely on a
passage in Plutarch's "Life of Julius
Caesar." The inclusion of the scene in
which the frenzied crowd tears apart
the poet who has the same name as
one of the conspirators shows the
tragic effects of mob rule. Is
Shakespeare also commenting on
the dangerous position in which
writers such as himself found
themselves when political turmoil
took hold? Shakespeare's company
was forced to explain their actions to
the Privy Council in 1601 when the
followers of Robert Devereux,
second Earl of Essex, had them
perform a version of *Richard II* on the
eve of his futile rebellion, an event
that led to the execution of the Earl
and many of his followers and the
imprisonment of others, such as
Shakespeare's first patron, Henry
Wriothesley, second Earl of
Southampton.

Cinna the Poet

Directly, [1] I am going to Caesar's funeral.

First Plebeian

As a friend or an enemy?   20

Cinna the Poet

As a friend.

Second Plebeian

That matter is answered directly.

Fourth Plebeian

For your dwelling—briefly.

Cinna the Poet

Briefly, I dwell by the Capitol.

Third Plebeian

Your name, sir, truly.   25

Cinna the Poet

Truly, my name is Cinna.

First Plebeian

Tear him to pieces! He's a conspirator!

Cinna the Poet

I am Cinna the Poet! I am Cinna the Poet!

Fourth Plebeian

Tear him for his bad verses! Tear him for his bad verses!

Cinna the Poet

I am not Cinna the conspirator!   30

Fourth Plebeian

It is no matter. His name's Cinna. Pluck but his name
out of his heart and turn him going. [2]

Third Plebeian

Tear him; tear him!

> [*The* **Plebeians** *beat* **Cinna the Poet**.]

Come, brands, ho, firebrands! To Brutus's, to Cassius's,
burn all! Some to Decius's house and some to Casca's.   35
Some to Ligarius'. Away, go!

> *All the* **Plebeians** *exit,* [*carrying* **Cinna the Poet**]. [2]

1 **Antony**, **Octavius**, and **Lepidus**

These three men made up the triumvirate that came to rule the Roman Empire. Shakespeare represents the forces opposing Brutus and Cassius as united until they turn on each other in *Antony and Cleopatra*, though the tensions among them are evident in this play. In fact, as Plutarch records, Antony and Octavius were bitter foes from the beginning, and Lepidus—a rather colorless figure here, but a more vigorous one in Plutarch—was invited to join them as a means of forcing them to unite. In the longer term the triumvirate proved to be a poisoned chalice for Antony and Lepidus, who became victims in turn of the single-minded ambition of Octavius.

2 *pricked*

Marked, with a small notation or pin prick

3 *Your brother*

Lucius Aemilius Paulus, a supporter of Brutus

4 *Publius*

Not the same man as Publius Cimber, whose enfranchisement the conspirators petitioned Caesar for in 3.1; Plutarch mentions a Publius Silicius who was condemned, though he was not a nephew of Antony.

5 *with a spot I damn him*

With this mark I condemn him to death.

6 *cut off some charge in legacies*

Diminish the amounts promised in Caesar's will

7 *threefold world divided*

The Roman Empire, comprised of Gaul, Italy (including Sicily and Sardinia), and Africa, to be divided between Antony, Octavius, and Lepidus

Act 4, Scene 1

Enter **Antony, Octavius,** *and* **Lepidus**. [1]

Antony

These many, then, shall die. Their names are pricked. [2]

Octavius

[*to* **Lepidus**] Your brother [3] too must die. Consent you,
  Lepidus?

Lepidus

I do consent—

Octavius

                              Prick him down, Antony.

Lepidus

the condition   Upon condition° Publius [4] shall not live,

Who is your sister's son, Mark Antony.   5

Antony

He shall not live. Look, with a spot I damn him. [5]

But, Lepidus, go you to Caesar's house.

Fetch the will hither, and we shall determine

How to cut off some charge in legacies. [6]

Lepidus

What, shall I find you here?   10

Octavius

Either   Or° here or at the Capitol.   **Lepidus** *exits.*

Antony

insignificant / unworthy   This is a slight,° unmeritable° man,

Fitting   Meet° to be sent on errands. Is it fit,

be   The threefold world divided, [7] he should stand°

One of the three to share it?

Octavius

                              So you thought him,   15

opinion   And took his voice° who should be pricked to die

1   *black sentence and proscription*
    Death sentences and confiscations

2   *divers sland'rous loads*
    All sorts of awkward accusations

3   *take we down his load and turn him off*
    **We unload what he has carried and
    turn him out to pasture.**

4   *apppoint him store of provender*
    Supply him with fodder

5   *that feeds / On objects, arts, and imita-
    tions, / Which, out of use and staled by
    other men, / Begin his fashion*
    **Who is amused by various foolish
    things, which others have long
    since tired of but which he thinks
    the height of fashion**

6   *levying powers*
    Raising an army

7   *straight make head*
    Immediately advance our forces

8   *Our best friends made*
    Other allies found

In our black sentence and proscription. [1]
Antony
Octavius, I have seen more days than you,
And, though we lay these honors on this man
To ease ourselves of divers sland'rous loads, [2]   20
He shall but bear them as the ass bears gold,
To groan and sweat under the business,
Either led or driven as we point the way;
want it   And, having brought our treasure where we will,°
Then take we down his load and turn him off, [3]   25
unburdened   Like to the empty° ass, to shake his ears
public pasture And graze in commons.°
Octavius
                                You may do your will,
experienced   But he's a tried° and valiant soldier.
Antony
So is my horse, Octavius, and for that
I do appoint him store of provender. [4]   30
It is a creature that I teach to fight,
turn around   To wind,° to stop, to run directly on,
corporeal; physical   His corporal° motion governed by my spirit,
degree   And, in some taste,° is Lepidus but so.
He must be taught and trained and bid go forth,   35
A barren-spirited fellow, one that feeds
On objects, arts, and imitations,
Which, out of use and staled by other men,
Begin his fashion. [5] Do not talk of him
tool   But as a property.° And now, Octavius,   40
Give attention to Listen° great things: Brutus and Cassius
Are levying powers. [6] We must straight make head. [7]
Therefore let our alliance be combined,
increased   Our best friends made, [8] our means stretched;°
immediately   And let us presently ° go sit in counsel   45

1   *How covert matters may be best*
    disclosed, / And open perils surest
    answerèd

    How (our enemies') secret plans
    may be successfully discovered and
    overt threats most safely
    countered

2   *at the stake / And bayed about with*
    many enemies

    The image comes from the practice
    of bearbaiting, a common
    Elizabethan entertainment in
    which a captive bear was tied to a
    stake and attacked by dogs.

How covert matters may be best disclosed,
And open perils surest answerèd. [1]

Octavius

Let us do so. For we are at the stake
And bayed about with many enemies; [2]
And some that smile have in their hearts, I fear,   50
evil intents   Millions of mischiefs.°   *They exit.*

1 *Give the word*

  **Pass on Brutus's command.
  (Lucilius passes Brutus's order
  down the chain of command.)**

2 *greets me well*

  Sends a worthy delegate

3 *In his own change or by ill officers*

  **I.e., either from a shift in Cassius's
  feelings or through the
  misconduct of his officers**

4 *be satisifed*

  Receive a full explanation

5 *familiar instances*

  Signs of friendship

Act 4, Scene 2

Drum. Enter **Brutus** *[with* **Lucius,**]**Lucilius**, *and the army.*
Titinius *and* **Pindarus** *meet them.*

Brutus

Halt!   Stand,° ho!

Lucilius

Give the word,[1] ho, and stand.

Brutus

What now, Lucilius? Is Cassius near?

Lucilius

He is at hand, and Pindarus is come

To do you salutation from his master.   5

Brutus

i.e., Cassius   He° greets me well.[2]—Your master, Pindarus,

In his own change or by ill officers[3]

justifiable   Hath given me some worthy° cause to wish

Things done undone, but if he be at hand,

I shall be satisfied.[4]

Pindarus

                I do not doubt   10

But that my noble master will appear

fully worthy   Such as he is, full° of regard and honor.

Brutus

He is not doubted.—A word, Lucilius.

[*takes* **Lucilius** *aside*] How he received you, let me be

informed   resolved.°

Lucilius

With courtesy and with respect enough,   15

But not with such familiar instances[5]

frank / conversation   Nor with such free° and friendly conference°

As he hath used of old.

1 *enforcèd ceremony*
   Unnatural formality

2 *hot at hand*
   Fast at the start

3 Low march within.
   The stage direction refers to the sounds of marching troops offstage.

4 *fall their crests*
   Lower their necks (no longer running hard)

5 *Sardis*
   The most important city of Lydia, an ancient nation in Asia Minor; see also 4.3.3.

6 *the horse in general*
   The entire cavalry

Brutus

Thou hast described

Always   A hot friend cooling. Ever° note, Lucilius,

When love begins to sicken and decay,   20

It useth an enforcèd ceremony. [1]

There are no tricks in plain and simple faith,

insincere   But hollow° men, like horses hot at hand, [2]

Make gallant show and promise of their mettle,

Low march within. [3]

But when they should endure the bloody spur,   25

nags   They fall their crests [4] and, like deceitful jades,°

Fail   Sink° in the trial. Comes his army on?

Lucilius

lodged   They mean this night in Sardis [5] to be quartered.°

The greater part, the horse in general, [6]

Are come with Cassius.

soldiers   *Enter* **Cassius** *and his powers.*°

Brutus

Hark! He is arrived.   30

calmly   March gently° on to meet him.

Cassius

Stand, ho!

Brutus

Stand, ho! Speak the word along!

First Soldier

Stand!

Second Soldier

Stand!   35

Third Soldier

Stand!

1   *sober form*

     Cold manner

2   *Lucius*

     The Folio prints "Lucilius" here and
     "Lucius" (for this text's *Lucilius*) at line
     52. This edition, with most others,
     has transposed the names since at
     4.3.127 Lucilius is guarding the door,
     and, as the new scene is continuous
     with 4.2, this must represent the
     original arrangement. Also, Lucius is
     clearly imagined as a boy (see the
     Folio stage direction at 4.3.157) and
     so a less likely choice for guarding
     than the soldier Lucilius.

Cassius

Most noble brother, you have done me wrong.

Brutus

Judge me, you gods! Wrong I mine enemies?

could And if not so, how should° I wrong a brother?

Cassius

Brutus, this sober form¹ of yours hides wrongs,　　40

And when you do them—

Brutus

calm　　　　　　　　　　　　　Cassius, be content.°

grievances Speak your griefs° softly. I do know you well.

Before the eyes of both our armies here,

between Which should perceive nothing but love from° us,

Let us not wrangle. Bid them move away;　　45

fully express Then in my tent, Cassius, enlarge° your griefs,

And I will give you audience.

Cassius

　　　　　　　　　　　　Pindarus,

troops Bid our commanders lead their charges° off

A little from this ground.

Brutus

Lucius,² do you the like, and let no man　　50

Come to our tent till we have done our conference.

Let Lucilius and Titinius guard our door.

They all exit, [but] **Brutus** *and* **Cassius** *remain.*

1   **Act 4, Scene 3**

The stage is not cleared after 4.2, as Brutus and Cassius remain, and therefore there is no need for a new scene. It has, however, become conventional to mark a new scene here because of the change of location from the field to the interior of Brutus's tent.

2   *praying on his side*

Pleading his case

3   *was slighted off*

Were ignored. A singular verb with a plural subject (especially if it can be imagined as a collection) was common usage.

4   *nice offense should bear his comment*

Trivial mistake should be criticized

5   *condemned to have an itching palm*

Accused of being greedy

6   *chastisement doth therefore hide his head*

For that reason no one will speak out against it

Act 4, Scene 3 [1]

Cassius

That you have wronged me doth appear in this:

disgraced   You have condemned and noted° Lucius Pella

For taking bribes here of the Sardians,

While   Wherein° my letters, praying on his side [2]

Because I knew the man, was slighted off. [3]   5

Brutus

You wronged yourself to write in such a case.

Cassius

fitting   In such a time as this it is not meet°

its   That every nice offense should bear his° comment. [4]

Brutus

Let me tell you, Cassius, you yourself

Are much condemned to have an itching palm, [5]   10

barter / positions of authority   To sell and mart° your offices° for gold

To undeservers.

Cassius

               I, "an itching palm"?

that it is only because   You know that° you are Brutus that speak this,

otherwise   Or, by the gods, this speech were else° your last.

Brutus

gives legitimacy to   The name of Cassius honors° this corruption,   15

And chastisement doth therefore hide his head. [6]

Cassius

"Chastisement"?

Brutus

Remember March; the ides of March remember.

Did not great Julius bleed for justice' sake?

What villain touched his body that did stab   20

And not for justice? What, shall one of us

That struck the foremost man of all this world

1   *But for supporting robbers*

    **Mainly for tolerating corruption (a
    motive for the assassination never
    before mentioned and contradicting
    Brutus's claim at 2.1.20–22)**

2   *the mighty space of our large honors*

    **The important positions in our
    power to assign**

3   *be a dog and bay the moon*

    **Proverbial for "engage in pointless
    activity"**

4   *hedge me in*

    Limit my authority

5   *Go to.*

    An expression of impatience

6   *Have mind upon your health.*

    **Look out for your safety (i.e., watch
    out).**

7   *give way and room to*

    Defer to and authorize

But for supporting robbers,[1] shall we now
Contaminate our fingers with base bribes
And sell the mighty space of our large honors[2]   25
i.e., money   For so much trash° as may be graspèd thus?
bark at   I had rather be a dog and bay° the moon[3]
Than such a Roman.

Cassius

torment   Brutus, bait° not me;
I'll not endure it. You forget yourself
To hedge me in.[4] I am a soldier, I,   30
Older in practice, abler than yourself
appointments   To make conditions.°

Brutus

Go to.[5] You are not, Cassius.

Cassius

I am.

Brutus

I say you are not.   35

Cassius

Provoke   Urge° me no more; I shall forget myself.
Test   Have mind upon your health.[6] Tempt° me no farther.

Brutus

insignificant   Away, slight° man!

Cassius

Is 't possible?

Brutus

                           Hear me, for I will speak.
anger   Must I give way and room to[7] your rash choler?°   40
Shall I be frighted when a madman stares?

Cassius

O ye gods, ye gods, must I endure all this?

Brutus

"All this"? Aye, more. Fret till your proud heart break.

1   *testy humor*

Hot-tempered mood

2   *digest the venom of your spleen, /*
Though it do split you

I.e., I will make you swallow your
own poisonous anger, even if it
makes you burst apart.

3   *learn of*

Most likely "learn from" (though
could possibly mean "learn the
existence of")

hot tempered | Go show your slaves how choleric° you are
slaves / flinch | And make your bondmen° tremble. Must I budge?° 45
defer to / cringe | Must I observe° you? Must I stand and crouch°
| Under your testy humor?[1] By the gods,
| You shall digest the venom of your spleen,
| Though it do split you.[2] For from this day forth,
| I'll use you for my mirth, yea, for my laughter, 50
irritable | When you are waspish.°

Cassius

Is it come to this?

Brutus

You say you are a better soldier.
boasting | Let it appear so. Make your vaunting° true,
| And it shall please me well. For mine own part,
| I shall be glad to learn of[3] noble men. 55

Cassius

You wrong me every way. You wrong me, Brutus:
I said an elder soldier, not a better.
Did I say "better"?

Brutus

If you did, I care not.

Cassius

dared / angered | When Caesar lived, he durst° not thus have moved° me.

Brutus

provoked | Peace, peace! You durst not so have tempted° him. 60

Cassius

I durst not?

Brutus

No.

Cassius

What, durst not tempt him?

Brutus

For your life you durst not.

1   *To lock such rascal counters*

    To keep such vile coins

2   *friends*

    Friendship was a key republican
    ideal, one that was supposed to
    cement personal and political
    loyalties to the state and
    emphasize the relative equality of
    Roman citizens. In the Roman
    Republic at its most successful,
    friends could debate on equal
    terms with each other and so iron
    out difficulties that threatened
    everyone's peace and happiness;
    here, however, the friendship itself
    is as flawed as the individuals who
    abuse it.

3   *He was but a fool that brought / My
    answer back.*

    I.e., the messenger is to blame for
    misrepresenting my response.

Cassius

Do not presume too much upon my love;

that which   I may do that° I shall be sorry for.   65

Brutus

You have done that you should be sorry for.

There is no terror, Cassius, in your threats,

integrity; honor   For I am armed so strong in honesty°

That they pass by me as the idle wind,

regard   Which I respect° not. I did send to you   70

For certain sums of gold, which you denied me,

For I can raise no money by vile means.

By Heaven, I had rather coin my heart

silver coins   And drop my blood for drachmas° than to wring

calloused   From the hard° hands of peasants their vile trash   75

dishonest means   By any indirection.° I did send

To you for gold to pay my legions,

Which you denied me. Was that done like Cassius?

Would   Should° I have answered Caius Cassius so?

When Marcus Brutus grows so covetous   80

To lock such rascal counters **1** from his friends, **2**

Be ready, gods, with all your thunderbolts.

Dash him to pieces!

Cassius

                              I denied you not.

Brutus

You did.

Cassius

I did not. He was but a fool that brought   85

broken   My answer back. **3** Brutus hath rived° my heart.

tolerate   A friend should bear° his friend's infirmities,

But Brutus makes mine greater than they are.

Brutus

use   I do not, till you practice° them on me.

1   *conned by rote*

    Memorized

2   *cast into my teeth*

    Throw in my face

3   *Dearer than Pluto's mine*

    **More precious than the mines of
    Pluto (possibly a reference to
    Plutus, the god of wealth, as
    opposed to *Pluto*, the god of the
    underworld; the two were often
    confused and conflated)**

4   *I, that denied thee gold, will give my heart.*

    **I, whom you accuse of denying you
    gold, will prove my loyalty by
    pledging my heart instead.**

5   *dishonor shall be humor*

    **I shall assume your insults to be no
    more than the product of a passing
    mood.**

Cassius

You love me not.

Brutus

                   I do not like your faults.   90

Cassius

A friendly eye could never see such faults.

Brutus

A flatterer's would not, though they do appear

As huge as high Olympus.

Cassius

Come, Antony, and young Octavius, come.

only   Revenge yourselves alone° on Cassius,   95

For Cassius is aweary of the world,

defied   Hated by one he loves, braved° by his brother,

Rebuked / slave   Checked° like a bondman,° all his faults observed,

Set in a notebook, learned, and conned by rote[1]

To cast into my teeth.[2] Oh, I could weep   100

My spirit from mine eyes. [*offering his dagger*] There

     is my dagger,

And here my naked breast, within, a heart

Dearer than Pluto's mine,[3] richer than gold.

If that thou be'st a Roman, take it forth.

I, that denied thee gold, will give my heart.[4]   105

Strike, as thou didst at Caesar, for I know

When thou didst hate him worst, thou loved'st him better

Than ever thou loved'st Cassius.

Brutus

                      Sheathe your dagger.

free reign   Be angry when you will; it shall have scope.°

Do what you will; dishonor shall be humor.[5]   110

i.e., Brutus   O Cassius, you are yokèd with a lamb°

That carries anger as the flint bears fire,

struck   Who, much enforcèd,° shows a hasty spark

1   *blood ill-tempered*

    Unbalanced disposition (with his
    humors, the elements that
    controlled physical and mental
    health, improperly mixed)

2   *rash humor which my mother gave me*

    Irascible temperament, inherited
    from my mother

3   *leave you so*

    Let it pass

immediately   And straight° is cold again.

Cassius

                Hath Cassius lived

nothing more than   To be but° mirth and laughter to his Brutus   115

When grief and blood ill-tempered[1] vexeth him?

Brutus

When I spoke that, I was ill-tempered too.

Cassius

Do you confess so much? Give me your hand.

Brutus

And my heart too.   [*They embrace.*]

Cassius

             O Brutus!

Brutus

                   What's the matter?

Cassius

Have not you love enough to bear with me   120

When that rash humor which my mother gave me[2]

Makes me forgetful?

Brutus

                Yes, Cassius. And from henceforth

overly critical   When you are over-earnest° with your Brutus,

He'll think your mother chides and leave you so.[3]

Enter a **Poet** [*followed by* **Lucilius** *and* **Titinius**].

Poet

Let me go in to see the generals.   125

There is some grudge between 'em. 'Tis not meet

They be alone.

Lucilius

              You shall not come to them.

1   *cynic*

    (1) rude fellow; (2) follower of the principles of Cynic philosophy, marked by, as Plutarch says, "contempt for ease"

2   *sirrah*

    Term of address usually used contemptuously or to an inferior

3   *I'll know his humor when he knows his time.*

    I'll endure his strange whims when he understands the appropriate time for them.

4   *jigging*

    Versifying (but always used pejoratively to describe awkward poetic effects)

5   *Companion*

    Fellow (said here with contempt)

6   *Messala*

    An officer in Brutus's army and member of an important Roman family.

Poet

stop Nothing but death shall stay° me.

Cassius

How now? What's the matter?

Poet

For shame, you generals! What do you mean?   130

Love and be friends as two such men should be,

For I have seen more years, I'm sure, than ye.

Cassius

Ha, ha, how vilely doth this cynic[1] rhyme!

Brutus

Insolent [*to* **Poet**] Get you hence, sirrah.[2] Saucy° fellow, hence!

Cassius

Bear with him, Brutus. 'Tis his fashion.   135

Brutus

I'll know his humor when he knows his time.[3]

What should the wars do with these jigging[4] fools?

—Companion,[5] hence!

Cassius

                                Away, away, be gone.

                                                Poet *exits.*

Brutus

Lucilius and Titinius, bid the commanders

Prepare to lodge their companies tonight.   140

Cassius

And come yourselves, and bring Messala[6] with you,

Immediately to us.   [**Lucilius** *and* **Titinius** *exit.*]

Brutus

                    [*calls*] Lucius, a bowl of wine!

Cassius

I did not think you could have been so angry.

1 *your philosophy*

Presumably a form of Stoicism, a
school of thought that emphasizes
self-discipline and restraint, but
see 5.1.102 and note.

2 *Portia is dead.*

Portia's death would probably
have been viewed in different ways
by different members of the
audience. Some may well have
accepted the world of the play and
viewed her suicide as a noble act by
a proud woman who lived before
Christian revelation. Others would
have seen it as a sign of the evils of
the pagan world and their false
philosophies, as all Christian faiths
condemned suicide as an act of
despair on the part of the
perpetrator, a lack of faith in God's
mercy and contempt for his
creation. Similarly, Brutus's muted
reaction may be a sign of his
detached, over-idealistic
character, or of his noble, Stoic
capacity to endure.

3 *Upon what sickness?*

Of what disease did she die?

4 *Impatient of*

Unable to endure

5 *for with her death / That tidings came*

Since along with the news of her
death came the news of the growth
of Antony's and Octavius's army

6 *swallowed fire*

Committed suicide by swallowing
hot coals

Brutus

as a result of O Cassius, I am sick of° many griefs.

Cassius

Of your philosophy[1] you make no use   145

in / misfortunes If you give place° to accidental evils.°

Brutus

No man bears sorrow better: Portia is dead.[2]

Cassius

What? Ha?° Portia?

Brutus

She is dead.

Cassius

being killed How 'scaped I killing° when I crossed you so?   150

grievous O insupportable and touching° loss!

Upon what sickness?[3]

Brutus

                    Impatient of[4] my absence

And grief that young Octavius with Mark Antony

Have made themselves so strong—for with her death

into a frenzy That tidings came[5]—with this she fell distract°   155

And, her attendants absent, swallowed fire.[6]

Cassius

And died so?

Brutus

            Even so.

Cassius

                    O ye immortal gods!

Enter Boy [**Lucius**] *with wine and tapers.*

Brutus

Speak no more of her.—Give me a bowl of wine.

—In this I bury all unkindness, Cassius.   *(drinks)*

1   *call in question*

Discuss; consider

2   *Philippi*

A city located in northeastern Greece, where the decisive battle between the forces of Antony and Octavius and those of Brutus and Cassius was fought in 42 B.C.

3   *proscription and bills of outlawry*

Executive order (for execution) and charge of criminal activity

Cassius

My heart is thirsty for that noble pledge.   160

overflow   —Fill, Lucius, till the wine o'erswell° the cup.   [*drinks*]

—I cannot drink too much of Brutus' love.

[**Lucius** *exits.*]

Enter **Titinius** *and* **Messala**.

Brutus

Come in, Titinius.—Welcome, good Messala!

Now sit we close about this taper here

And call in question¹ our necessities.   [*They sit.*]   165

Cassius

Portia, art thou gone?

Brutus

No more, I pray you.

—Messala, I have here receivèd letters

That young Octavius and Mark Antony

army   Come down upon us with a mighty power,°

Directing Bending° their expedition toward Philippi.²   170

Messala

substance Myself have letters of the selfsame tenor.°

Brutus

With what addition?

Messala

That by proscription and bills of outlawry,³

Octavius, Antony, and Lepidus

Have put to death an hundred senators.   175

Brutus

Therein our letters do not well agree:

Mine speak of seventy senators that died

By their proscriptions, Cicero being one.

1   *Nor nothing in your letters writ of her?*

Nor was anything written about her
in the letters you did receive?

2   *Nothing, Messala.*

Brutus's professions of ignorance
about Portia's death in lines 182–187
seem to contradict what he has just
told Cassius, but they are in keeping
with Brutus's resolve to *Speak no more
of her* (4.3.158) and allow him to
demonstrate his self-control; some
scholars, however, believe this
represents a version of the
announcement of Portia's death
that was intended for deletion but
printed by mistake.

3   *in art*

In theory (i.e., the Stoic principles
of fortitude)

Cassius

Cicero one?

Messala

           Cicero is dead,

And by that order of proscription.   180

[*to* **Brutus**] Had you your letters from your wife, my

    lord?

Brutus

No, Messala.

Messala

Nor nothing in your letters writ of her?[1]

Brutus

Nothing, Messala.[2]

Messala

                 That, methinks, is strange.

Brutus

anything   Why ask you? Hear you aught° of her in yours?   185

Messala

No, my lord.

Brutus

Now, as you are a Roman, tell me true.

Messala

Then, like a Roman, bear the truth I tell,

For certain she is dead, and by strange manner.

Brutus

Why, farewell, Portia. We must die, Messala.   190

i.e., some day   With meditating that she must die once,°

I have the patience to endure it now.

Messala

Even so great men great losses should endure.

Cassius

I have as much of this in art[3] as you,

But yet my nature could not bear it so.   195

1   *to our work alive*

    To the tasks that face us now

2   *forced affection*

    Compelled allegiance

3   *Under your pardon.*

    I.e., with your permission, let me
    continue.

4   *tried the utmost*

    Strained the limits

Brutus

Well, to our work alive.[1] What do you think

immediately   Of marching to Philippi presently?°

Cassius

I do not think it good.

Brutus

                                Your reason?

Cassius

                                        This it is:

'Tis better that the enemy seek us;

supplies   So shall he waste his means,° weary his soldiers,   200

harm   Doing himself offense,° whilst we, lying still,

Are full of rest, defense, and nimbleness.

Brutus

necessity   Good reasons must of force° give place to better.

i.e., place   The people 'twixt Philippi and this ground°

Do stand but in a forced affection,[2]   205

supplies   For they have grudged us contribution.°

past   The enemy, marching along by° them,

their men   By them° shall make a fuller number up,

reinforced   Come on refreshed, new-added,° and encouraged,

i.e., Antony's army   From which advantage shall we cut him° off   210

If at Philippi we do face him there,

i.e., Philippians   These people° at our back.

Cassius

                        Hear me, good brother—

Brutus

Under your pardon.[3] You must note beside

That we have tried the utmost[4] of our friends.

Our legions are brim-full; our cause is ripe.   215

The enemy increaseth every day.

We, at the height, are ready to decline.

There is a tide in the affairs of men

1   *at the flood*
     The peak of high tide

2   *with your will*
     As you wish

3   *will niggard*
     Sparingly satisfy

Which, taken at the flood,¹ leads on to fortune;

Missed   Omitted,° all the voyage of their life   220

confined   Is bound° in shallows and in miseries.

On such a full sea are we now afloat,

And we must take the current when it serves

investments   Or lose our ventures.°

Cassius

               Then, with your will,² go on.

We'll along ourselves and meet them at Philippi.   225

Brutus

The deep of night is crept upon our talk,

And nature must obey necessity,

Which we will niggard³ with a little rest.

There is no more to say?

Cassius

             No more. Good night.

depart   Early tomorrow will we rise and hence.°   *[They stand.]* 230

Enter **Lucius**.

Brutus

Lucius, My gown.   **[Lucius** *exits.]*

         —Farewell, good Messala.

—Good night, Titinius.—Noble, noble Cassius,

Good night and good repose.

Cassius

i.e., brother-in-law   O my dear brother,°

This was an ill beginning of the night.

Never come such division 'tween our souls;   235

Let it not, Brutus.

Enter **Lucius** *with the gown.*

1   *instrument*

   Most likely a lute

2   *knave*

   I.e., lad; used affectionately here

3   *o'erwatched*

   Exhausted from staying awake

4   *watch your pleasure*

   Await your orders

Brutus

Everything is well.

Cassius

Good night, my lord.

Brutus

Good night, good brother.

Titinius, Messala

Good night, Lord Brutus.   240

Brutus

Farewell, everyone.

                    [**Cassius**, **Titinius**, and **Messala**] exit.

Give me the gown. Where is thy instrument? [1]

Lucius

Here in the tent.

Brutus

                        What, thou speak'st drowsily?

Poor knave, [2] I blame thee not. Thou art o'erwatched. [3]

Call Claudio and some other of my men;   245

I'll have them sleep on cushions in my tent.

Lucius

Varrus and Claudio!

                    Enter **Varrus** and **Claudio**.

Varrus

Calls my lord?

Brutus

I pray you, sirs, lie in my tent and sleep.

It may be I shall raise you by and by   250

On business to my brother Cassius.

Varrus

stand watch   So please you, we will stand° and watch your pleasure. [4]

1   *otherwise bethink me*

Change my mind

2   *sought for so*

Looked for so hard

3   *murd'rous slumber*

Sleep is *murd'rous* because it marks "the death of each day's life" (*Macbeth* 2.2.41).

4   *Lay'st thou thy leaden mace*

The image is of sleep as an arresting officer touching the shoulder of the person he apprehends with his staff of office (*mace*), though oddly reversing the valence of the image in the previous line where sleep is *murd'rous*.

Brutus

I will not have it so. Lie down, good sirs.

It may be I shall otherwise bethink me. [1]

—Look, Lucius, here's the book I sought for so; [2]   255

I put it in the pocket of my gown.

                    [**Varrus** *and* **Claudio** *lie down.*]

Lucius

I was sure your Lordship did not give it me.

Brutus

Bear with me, good boy; I am much forgetful.

Canst thou hold up thy heavy eyes awhile

play / tune And touch° thy instrument a strain° or two?   260

Lucius

if Aye, my lord, an° 't please you.

Brutus

                         It does, my boy.

I trouble thee too much, but thou art willing.

Lucius

It is my duty, sir.

Brutus

capacity I should not urge thy duty past thy might.°

i.e., bodies I know young bloods° look for a time of rest.   265

Lucius

I have slept, my lord, already.

Brutus

It was well done, and thou shalt sleep again.

I will not hold thee long. If I do live,

I will be good to thee.

            Music and a song [*, then* **Lucius** *sleeps*].

This is a sleepy tune. O murd'rous slumber, [3]   270

Lay'st thou thy leaden mace [4] upon my boy

That plays thee music?—Gentle knave, good night.

I will not do thee so much wrong to wake thee.

1   Enter the **Ghost** of Caesar.

Ghosts frequently appeared on the
early modern stage. Caesar's
appearance as a ghost here
reinforces our sense of the pagan,
alien world of *Julius Caesar*, one in
which the characters are constantly
undermined in their efforts by forces
beyond their control, but it also
shows the futility of Brutus's desire
merely to kill *Caesar's spirit* (2.1.169).
Plutarch reports the appearance of
the Ghost, saying that it "showed
plainly the gods were offended with
the murder of Caesar." In Shakespeare's play, it could merely be
a projection of Brutus's guilty
conscience. It is a *monstrous
apparition*, that is, an unnatural
appearance that could be an actual
ghost, a hallucination, or some sort
of supernatural creature (*some god,
some angel, or some devil*), but it is an
evil spirit that predicts Brutus's defeat
and death.

2   *will*

Brutus's shift here to *will* from *shall*
in line 287 marks a change from
mere uncertainty about the future
to an acceptance of the
inevitability of his fate.

If thou dost nod, thou break'st thy instrument.
I'll take it from thee, and, good boy, good night.   275
—Let me see, let me see. Is not the leaf turned down
Where I left reading? Here it is, I think.

*Enter the **Ghost** of Caesar.* [1]

How ill this taper burns!—Ha, who comes here?
I think it is the weakness of mine eyes
That shapes this monstrous apparition.   280
toward   It comes upon° me.—Art thou any thing?
Art thou some god, some angel, or some devil
stand on end That mak'st my blood cold and my hair to stare?°
Speak to me what thou art.
Ghost

                                 Thy evil spirit, Brutus.
Brutus

Why com'st thou?   285
Ghost

To tell thee thou shalt see me at Philippi.
Brutus

Well, then I shall see thee again?
Ghost

Aye, at Philippi.
Brutus

Why, I will [2] see thee at Philippi, then.   [**Ghost** *exits.*]
Now that   Now° I have taken heart, thou vanishest.   290
Ill spirit, I would hold more talk with thee.
—Boy, Lucius! Varrus! Claudio! Sirs, awake!
Claudio!
Lucius

out of tune The strings, my lord, are false.°

1 *commend me*

Deliver my greeting

Brutus

He thinks he still is at his instrument.   295
Lucius, awake!

Lucius

My lord?

Brutus

Didst thou dream, Lucius, that thou so cried'st out?

Lucius

My lord, I do not know that I did cry.

Brutus

Yes, that thou didst. Didst thou see anything?   300

Lucius

Nothing, my lord.

Brutus

Sleep again, Lucius.—Sirrah Claudio!
[*to* **Varrus**] Fellow thou, awake!

Varrus

                                    My lord?

Claudio

                                         My lord?

Brutus

Why did you so cry out, sirs, in your sleep?

Varrus, Claudio

[*rising*] Did we, my lord?

Brutus

                         Aye. Saw you anything?   305

Varrus

No, my lord, I saw nothing.

Claudio

                    Nor I, my lord.

Brutus

Go and commend me[1] to my brother Cassius.

1   *set on his powers betimes before*

Send his forces early, before mine

Bid him set on his powers betimes before, [1]
And we will follow.

Varrus, Claudio

It shall be done, my lord.

They exit.

1　*come down*

Attack

2　*am in their bosoms*

Know their thoughts

3　*could be content / To visit other places*

Wish they were elsewhere

4　*come down / With fearful bravery*

Attack with a terrifying show of courage

5　*bloody sign of battle*

Signal to begin the battle (which Plutarch says was a "scarlet coat")

Act 5, Scene 1

Enter **Octavius**, **Antony**, *and their army.*

Octavius

Now, Antony, our hopes are answerèd.

You said the enemy would not come down[1]

stay in But keep° the hills and upper regions.

forces It proves not so. Their battles° are at hand.

confront They mean to warn° us at Philippi here,   5

Answering before we do demand of them.

Antony

Tut, I am in their bosoms,[2] and I know

Why Wherefore° they do it. They could be content

To visit other places,[3] and come down

display With fearful bravery,[4] thinking by this face°   10

To fasten in our thoughts that they have courage.

But 'tis not so.

Enter a **Messenger**.

Messenger

             Prepare you, generals.

The enemy comes on in gallant show.

Their bloody sign of battle[5] is hung out,

And something to be done immediately.   15

Antony

army / warily Octavius, lead your battle° softly° on,

Upon the left hand of the even field.

Octavius

Upon the right hand, I. Keep thou the left.

Antony

oppose / crucial moment Why do you cross° me in this exigent?°

243

1 March

The stage direction indicates a movement of troops. See 4.2.24 and note.

2 *answer on their charge*

Confront them when they attack

3 *Make forth.*

Go ahead

4 *posture of your blows*

How you will fight

5 *your words*

I.e., Antony's protestations of friendship after Caesar's death

6 *Hybla*

Town in Sicily known for its honey

Octavius

I do not cross you, but I will do so.   *March.*[1] 20

> *Drum. Enter* **Brutus**, **Cassius**, *and their army* [*with*
> **Lucilius**, **Titinius**, *and* **Messala**].

Brutus

a conference They stand and would have parley.°

Cassius

go out Stand fast, Titinius. We must out° and talk.

Octavius

Mark Antony, shall we give sign of battle?

Antony

No, Caesar, we will answer on their charge.[2]

Make forth.[3] The generals would have some words.   25

Octavius

[*to his officers*] Stir not until the signal.

Brutus

Words before blows. Is it so, countrymen?

Octavius

Not that we love words better, as you do.

Brutus

Good words are better than bad strokes, Octavius.

Antony

In your bad strokes, Brutus, you give good words.   30

Witness the hole you made in Caesar's heart,

Crying "Long live, hail, Caesar!"

Cassius

                         Antony,

The posture of your blows[4] are yet unknown.

as for But for° your words,[5] they rob the Hybla[6] bees

And leave them honeyless.   35

1 *showed your teeth*

   Grinned

2 *proof*

   test (of the argument in battle)

3 *goes up*

   Will be sheathed

4 *till another Caesar / Have added slaughter to*

   Till Octavius too is slain by

5 *Unless thou bring'st them with thee*

   Unless they are your own

Antony

Not stingless too?

Brutus

Oh, yes, and soundless too.

For you have stol'n their buzzing, Antony,

threaten And very wisely threat° before you sting.

Antony

Villains, you did not so when your vile daggers   40

Hacked one another in the sides of Caesar.

You showed your teeth [1] like apes, and fawned like
    hounds,

slaves And bowed like bondmen° kissing Caesar's feet,

Whilst damnèd Casca, like a cur, behind

Struck Caesar on the neck. O you flatterers!   45

Cassius

"Flatterers"?—Now, Brutus, thank yourself.

This tongue had not offended so today

had his way If Cassius might have ruled.°

Octavius

issue at hand Come, come, the cause.° If arguing make us sweat,

The proof [2] of it will turn to redder drops.   50

Look, I draw a sword against conspirators.   [*He draws.*]

When think you that the sword goes up [3] again?

Never till Caesar's three and thirty wounds

Be well avenged, or till another Caesar

Have added slaughter to [4] the sword of traitors.   55

Brutus

Caesar, thou canst not die by traitors' hands

Unless thou bring'st them with thee. [5]

Octavius

                So I hope;

I was not born to die on Brutus' sword.

1 *a masquer and a reveler*

I.e., Antony (Plutarch reports that in Antony's house they "did nothing but feast, dance, and mask"; see also 1.2.204–205 and 2.2.116.)

2 *swell billow*

Surge waves

3 *on the hazard*

Being risked

4 *As Pompey was*

At Pharsalia in 48 B.C., Pompey was led against his better judgment to commit his troops to battle and was defeated by Caesar.

Brutus

Oh, if thou wert the noblest of thy strain,

Young man, thou couldst not die more honorable.   60

Cassius

foolish / i.e., Octavius   A peevish° schoolboy,° worthless of such honor,

Joined with a masquer and a reveler! [1]

Antony

Old Cassius still.

Octavius

Come, Antony, away.

—Defiance, traitors, hurl we in your teeth.

If you dare fight today, come to the field.   65

the appetite for it   If not, when you have stomachs.°

Octavius, **Antony**, *and army exit.*

Cassius

ship   Why now, blow wind, swell billow,[2] and swim bark!°

The storm is up and all is on the hazard. [3]

Brutus

Ho, Lucilius; hark, a word with you.

Lucilius

My lord?   [**Brutus** *and* **Lucilius** *talk aside.*]   70

Cassius

Messala!

Messala

What says my General?

Cassius

on   Messala, this is my birthday, as° this very day

Was Cassius born. Give me thy hand, Messala.

Be thou my witness that against my will,   75

gamble   As Pompey was, [4] am I compelled to set°

Upon one battle all our liberties.

1   *held Epicurus strong*

Believed in the philosophy of
Epicurus (who insisted the gods took
no role in human affairs, and thus
they dismissed all belief in omens)

2   *former ensign*

Most forward banner (i.e., the flag
carried by the vanguard of the
army)

3   *give up the ghost*

I.e., die

4   *rests still*

Remain always

5   *reason with*

Think about

6   *that philosophy*

In his disapproval of suicide,
Brutus marks his distance from
traditional Stoicism. Indeed
Plutarch says that he was of
"Plato's sect" (Plato's *Phaedo*
rejects suicide), nonetheless
Brutus clearly embraced many
Stoical principles. As he confronts
the possibility of his defeat,
however, he admits the limits of
his *patience / To stay the providence of
some high powers* (see lines 107–113).

You know that I held Epicurus strong[1]
And his opinion. Now I change my mind,

predict the future   And partly credit things that do presage.°   80
Coming from Sardis, on our former ensign[2]
Two mighty eagles fell, and there they perched,
Gorging and feeding from our soldiers' hands,

accompanied   Who to Philippi here consorted° us.
This morning are they fled away and gone,   85
And in their steads do ravens, crows, and kites
Fly o'er our heads and downward look on us

As if   As° we were sickly prey. Their shadows seem

ominous   A canopy most fatal° under which
Our army lies, ready to give up the ghost.[3]   90
Messala
Believe not so.
Cassius

only   I but° believe it partly,
For I am fresh of spirit and resolved

resolutely   To meet all perils very constantly.°
                        [**Brutus** *returns with* **Lucilius**.]
Brutus
                                    Even so, Lucilius.
Cassius
Now, most noble Brutus,

i.e., May the   The° gods today stand friendly that we may,   95

Friends   Lovers° in peace, lead on our days to age,
But, since the affairs of men rests still[4] incertain,
Let's reason with[5] the worst that may befall:
If we do lose this battle, then is this
The very last time we shall speak together.   100
What are you then determinèd to do?
Brutus
Even by the rule of that philosophy[6]

1   *Cato*

     Portia's father; see 2.1.295 and
     LONGER NOTE on page 284.

2   *The time of life*

     The natural course of one's life

By which I did blame Cato[1] for the death

why Which he did give himself—I know not how,°

But I do find it cowardly and vile,   105

happen For fear of what might fall,° so to prevent

The time of life,[2] arming myself with patience

await To stay° the providence of some high powers

That govern us below.

Cassius

                        Then if we lose this battle

You are contented to be led in triumph   110

Through Thorough° the streets of Rome?

Brutus

No, Cassius, no. Think not, thou noble Roman,

That ever Brutus will go bound to Rome;

He bears too great a mind. But this same day

Must end that work the ides of March begun,   115

And whether we shall meet again I know not;

Therefore our everlasting farewell take.

Forever and forever farewell, Cassius.

If we do meet again, why, we shall smile.

If not, why then this parting was well made.   120

Cassius

Forever and forever farewell, Brutus.

If we do meet again, we'll smile indeed.

If not, 'tis true this parting was well made.

Brutus

Why then, lead on. Oh, that a man might know

The end of this day's business ere it come!   125

But it sufficeth that the day will end,

And then the end is known.—Come, ho! Away!

                                                They exit.

1   Alarum

Trumpet call signaling troops to battle

2   *the legions on the other side*

I.e., the soldiers under Cassius's command

3   *But cold demeanor*

A lack of fighting spirit

4   *gives them the overthrow*

Will defeat them

Act 5, Scene 2

Alarum.[1] *Enter* **Brutus** *and* **Messala**.

Brutus

orders   Ride, ride, Messala; ride and give these bills°
         Unto the legions on the other side.[2]   *[gives him papers]*
                                        Loud alarum.

         Let them set on at once, for I perceive

forces   But cold demeanor[3] in Octavius' wing,°
         And sudden push gives them the overthrow.[4]   5

i.e., Cassius's troops   Ride, ride, Messala. Let them° all come down.
                              They exit [separately].

1   *the villains*

I.e., our own soldiers

2   *mine own*

My own men

3   *even with*

As quick as

Act 5, Scene 3

Alarums. Enter **Cassius** *and* **Titinius**.

Cassius
Oh, look, Titinius, look: the villains [1] fly!
Myself have to mine own [2] turned enemy.

flag bearer This ensign° here of mine was turning back;
i.e., the flag I slew the coward and did take it° from him.

Titinius
O Cassius, Brutus gave the word too early,   5
Who, having some advantage on Octavius,
looting Took it too eagerly. His soldiers fell to spoil,°
Whilst we by Antony are all enclosed.

Enter **Pindarus**.

Pindarus
Fly further off, my lord; fly further off.
Mark Antony is in your tents, my lord.   10
Fly, therefore, noble Cassius; fly far off.

Cassius
This hill is far enough.—Look, look, Titinius.
Are those my tents where I perceive the fire?

Titinius
They are, my lord.

Cassius
                        Titinius, if thou lovest me,
dig Mount thou my horse, and hide° thy spurs in him   15
Till he have brought thee up to yonder troops
back And here° again, that I may rest assured
Whether yond troops are friend or enemy.

Titinius
I will be here again, even with [3] a thought.   *He exits.*

1   [**Pindarus** exits.]

It isn't clear whether Pindarus exits
and speaks his lines from off stage
or if he reappears above in a gallery
and can be seen by the audience.
No doubt it varies depending on
the resources of the theater in
which the play is performed.

2   *This day I breathèd first.*

I.e., today is my birthday

3   *make to him on the spur*

Approach him at a gallop

4   *Parthia*

A country in what is now northern
Iran, invaded by Rome in 52 B.C.

5   *swore thee*

Made you swear

Cassius

Go, Pindarus; get higher on that hill.   20

weak / Observe   My sight was ever thick.° Regard° Titinius,

note; notice   And tell me what thou not'st° about the field.

                                        [**Pindarus** *exits.*][1]

This day I breathèd first.[2] Time is come round,

And where I did begin, there shall I end.

full circle   My life is run his compass.° [*to* **Pindarus**] Sirrah, what

          news?   25

Pindarus

[*within*] O my lord!

Cassius

What news?

Pindarus

[*within*] Titinius is enclosèd round about

With horsemen that make to him on the spur,[3]

Yet he spurs on. Now they are almost on him.   30

alight; dismount   —Now, Titinius!—Now some light.° Oh, he lights too.

captured   He's ta'en.°   *Shout* [*within*].

          And, hark! They shout for joy.

Cassius

Come down; behold no more.

Oh, coward that I am, to live so long

To see my best friend ta'en before my face!   35

          Pindarus *enters.*

Come hither, sirrah.

In Parthia[4] did I take thee prisoner.

i.e., in return for the saving   And then I swore thee,[5] saving° of thy life,

That whatsoever I did bid thee do,

Thou shouldst attempt it. Come now, keep thine oath.   40

1 *Stand not*

Do not wait

3 *Durst I have done my will*

If I had dared do what I wanted

3 *change*

An exchange of fortune

Now be a free man, and with this good sword,

penetrate　　　That ran through Caesar's bowels, search° this bosom.

sword handle　　Stand not[1] to answer. Here take thou the hilts°

And, when my face is covered, as 'tis now,

Guide thou the sword.　　　　　[**Pindarus** *stabs* **Cassius**.]

　　　　　　　　　　　　Caesar, thou art revenged,　　45

Even with the sword that killed thee.　　　　[*He dies.*]

Pindarus

So I am free. Yet would not so have been,

Durst I have done my will.[2] O Cassius,

Far from this country Pindarus shall run,

Where never Roman shall take note of him.　　　[*He exits.*]　　50

　　　　　　　Enter **Titinius** *and* **Messala**.

Messala

It is but change,[3] Titinius, for Octavius

Is overthrown by noble Brutus' power,

As Cassius' legions are by Antony.

Titinius

These tidings will well comfort Cassius.

Messala

Where did you leave him?

Titinius

　　　　　　　　　　　　All disconsolate,　　55

With Pindarus his bondman on this hill.

Messala

i.e., Cassius　　Is not that he° that lies upon the ground?

Titinius

He lies not like the living. O my heart!

Messala

Is not that he?

1   *Mistrust of my success*

    Doubt about the outcome of my mission

2   *the mother*

    I.e., the melancholic mind that gave birth to *error, melancholy's child*

3   *darts envenomèd*

    Poisoned arrows

Titinius

　　　　　　No, this was he, Messala,
But Cassius is no more. O setting sun,　　　　　60
As in thy red rays thou dost sink tonight,
So in his red blood Cassius' day is set.
The sun of Rome is set. Our day is gone.
Clouds, dews, and dangers come. Our deeds are done.
Mistrust of my success¹ hath done this deed.　　　65

Messala

Mistrust of good success hath done this deed.
O hateful error, melancholy's child,
impressionable　Why dost thou show to the apt° thoughts of men
The things that are not? O error, soon conceived,
Thou never com'st unto a happy birth　　　　　70
But kill'st the mother² that engendered thee!

Titinius

What, Pindarus! Where art thou, Pindarus?

Messala

Seek him, Titinius, whilst I go to meet
The noble Brutus, thrusting this report
Into his ears. I may say "thrusting" it,　　　　75
For piercing steel and darts envenomèd³
Shall be as welcome to the ears of Brutus
As tidings of this sight.

Titinius

Hurry　　　　　　　　Hie° you, Messala,
meanwhile　And I will seek for Pindarus the while.°　[**Messala** *exits.*]
Why didst thou send me forth, brave Cassius?　　80
Did I not meet thy friends? And did not they
Put on my brows this wreath of victory
And bid me give it thee? Didst thou not hear their shouts?
Alas, thou hast misconstrued everything!

1   *own proper*

    Very own

2   Low

    Soft (suggesting battles in the distance)

3   *Look whe'er he have not*

    See if he hasn't

But, hold thee, take this garland on thy brow.   85
Thy Brutus bid me give it thee, and I
Will do his bidding. [*lays wreath on* **Cassius**'s *head*]
    Brutus, come apace,
And see how I regarded Caius Cassius.
i.e., committing suicide —By your leave, gods, this° is a Roman's part.
Come, Cassius' sword, and find Titinius' heart.   *Dies.* 90

Alarum. Enter **Brutus**, **Messala**, *young* **Cato**, **Strato**,
Volumnius, **Lucilius**, [**Labio**, *and* **Flavius**].

Brutus
Where, where, Messala, doth his body lie?
Messala
Lo, yonder, and Titinius mourning it.
Brutus
Titinius' face is upward.
Cato
                                He is slain.
Brutus
O Julius Caesar, thou art mighty yet!
Thy spirit walks abroad and turns our swords   95
In our own proper¹ entrails.   *Low² alarums.*
Cato
                                Brave Titinius!
whether Look whe'er° he have not³ crowned dead Cassius.
Brutus
Are yet two Romans living such as these?
—The last of all the Romans, fare thee well!
It is impossible that ever Rome   100
equal Should breed thy fellow.°—Friends, I owe more tears
To this dead man than you shall see me pay.

1 *Thasos*

   **An island off the coast of Thrace,
   near Philippi.**

2 *young Cato*

   **The son of Marcus Porcius Cato
   and thus Portia's brother; see
   2.1.295 and note.**

3 *set our battles on*

   Get our forces ready

—I shall find time, Cassius; I shall find time.

—Come, therefore, and to Thasos[1] send his body.

His funerals shall not be in our camp,   105

dishearten   Lest it discomfort° us. Lucilius, come.

And come, young Cato.[2] Let us to the field.

Labio and Flavius, set our battles on.[3]

'Tis three o'clock, and, Romans, yet ere night

We shall try fortune in a second fight.   110

              They exit [with the bodies].

1 **Lucilius**

There is no speech prefix here in
the Folio, but Lucilius's pretense is
exposed by Antony at line 26 (and
is discussed in Plutarch).

2 *Only I yield*

I only yield in order

3 *There is so much that thou wilt kill*
me straight.

Many editors take this to mean
"Here is so so much gold to ensure you
kill me immediately (*straight*)" and
add a stage direction [*offering money*].
But remembering that Lucilius is
pretending to be Brutus, the
meaning is more likely "(as I am
Brutus), you have much reason to kill
me right now."

Act 5, Scene 4

Alarum. Enter **Brutus**, **Messala**, **Cato**, **Lucilius**, *and*
Flavius.

Brutus

Still Yet,° countrymen, oh, yet hold up your heads!

                         [**Brutus**, **Messala**, *and* **Flavius** *exit*.]

Cato

What bastard doth not? Who will go with me?

I will proclaim my name about the field.

I am the son of Marcus Cato, ho,

A foe to tyrants, and my country's friend.   5

I am the son of Marcus Cato, ho!

           Enter [**Antony** *and* **Octavius**'] **Soldiers** *and fight*.

Lucilius[1]

And I am Brutus, Marcus Brutus, I,

Brutus, my country's friend. Know me for Brutus!

                          [**Soldiers** *kill* **Cato**.]

O young and noble Cato, art thou down?

Why, now thou diest as bravely as Titinius,   10

And mayst be honored, being Cato's son.

First Soldier

Yield, or thou diest.

Lucilius

                Only I yield[2] to die.

There is so much that thou wilt kill me straight.[3]

Kill Brutus and be honored in his death.

First Soldier

We must not. A noble prisoner!   15

1 *like himself*

I.e., true to his nature

2 *is chanced*

Has turned out

Second Soldier

Make room   Room,° ho! Tell Antony Brutus is ta'en.

First Soldier

I'll tell the news. Here comes the General.

Brutus is ta'en; Brutus is ta'en, my lord.

Antony

Where is he?

Lucilius

Safe, Antony. Brutus is safe enough.   20

I dare assure thee that no enemy

Shall ever take alive the noble Brutus.

The gods defend him from so great a shame!

either   When you do find him, or° alive or dead,

He will be found like Brutus, like himself. [1]   25

Antony

[*to* **First Soldier**] This is not Brutus, friend, but, I assure you,

A prize no less in worth. Keep this man safe.

Give him all kindness. I had rather have

Such men my friends than enemies. Go on

And see whe'er Brutus be alive or dead,   30

And bring us word unto Octavius' tent

How everything is chanced. [2]   *They exit* [*separately*].

1   *showed the torchlight*

Statilius, in Plutarch, was sent to
check on Cassius's success and to
"lift up a torch-light in the air" if all
was well; he signaled, but was soon
after captured and then killed.

2   *or ta'en*

Either taken

Act 5, Scene 5

Enter **Brutus**, **Dardanius**, **Clitus**, **Strato**, *and*
Volumnius.

Brutus

Come, poor remains of friends; rest on this rock.

Clitus

Statilius showed the torchlight¹ but, my lord,
He came not back. He is or ta'en² or slain.

Brutus

Sit thee down, Clitus. Slaying is the word.
It is a deed in fashion. Hark thee, Clitus.   [*whispers to him*]   5

Clitus

What, I, my lord? No, not for all the world.

Brutus

Quiet   Peace° then! No words.

Clitus

I'll rather kill myself.

Brutus

Hark thee, Dardanius. [*whispers to him*]

Dardanius

Shall I do such a deed?

Clitus

O Dardanius!

Dardanius

O Clitus!   10

Clitus

[*aside to* **Dardanius**] What ill request did Brutus make to
thee?

Dardanius

[*aside to* **Clitus**] To kill him, Clitus. Look, he meditates.

1 *List a word.*

   Listen for a moment.

2 *beat us to the pit*

   **Driven us to the grave (*pit* literally
   referring to a trap for animals)**

Clitus

Now is that noble vessel full of grief,

That it runs over even at his eyes.

Brutus

Come hither, good Volumnius. List a word. [1]   15

Volumnius

What says my lord?

Brutus

          Why this, Volumnius:

The ghost of Caesar hath appeared to me

separate   Two several° times by night: at Sardis once,

And this last night here in Philippi fields.

I know my hour is come.

Volumnius

          Not so, my lord.   20

Brutus

Nay, I am sure it is, Volumnius.

Thou see'st the world, Volumnius, how it goes.

Our enemies have beat us to the pit. [2]   *Low alarums.*

It is more worthy to leap in ourselves

Than tarry till they push us. Good Volumnius,   25

Thou know'st that we two went to school together.

Even for that our love of old, I prithee,

handle   Hold thou my sword hilts,° whilst I run on it.

Volumnius

duty / continues   That's not an office° for a friend, my lord.   *Alarum still.°*

Clitus

Fly, fly, my lord. There is no tarrying here.   30

Brutus

Farewell to you,—and you,—and you, Volumnius.

—Strato, thou hast been all this while asleep.

1   *but he was*

   Who was not

2   *attain unto*

   Achieve

3   *fare you well at once*

   Leave with no further fuss.

4   *Night hangs upon mine eyes.*

   I.e., I am exhausted.

5   Retreat

   **The trumpet call signalling the end
   of an attack**

Farewell to thee too, Strato. —Countrymen,
My heart doth joy that yet in all my life
I found no man but he was[1] true to me.   35
I shall have glory by this losing day
More than Octavius and Mark Antony
By this vile conquest shall attain unto.[2]
So fare you well at once,[3] for Brutus' tongue
Hath almost ended his life's history.   40
Night hangs upon mine eyes.[4] My bones would rest
That have but labored to attain this hour.

        Alarum. Cry within "Fly, fly, fly!"

Clitus
Fly, my lord, fly.

Brutus
        Hence. I will follow.

        [**Clitus**, **Dardanius**, *and* **Volumnius** *exit.*]

I prithee, Strato, stay thou by thy lord.

reputation   Thou art a fellow of a good respect.°   45
taste   Thy life hath had some smatch° of honor in it.
Hold then my sword and turn away thy face
While I do run upon it. Wilt thou, Strato?

Strato
Give me your hand first. Fare you well, my lord.

Brutus
Farewell, good Strato. [*runs on his sword*] Caesar, now be
    still.   50
I killed not thee with half so good a will.   [*He*] *dies.*

        Alarum. Retreat.[5] *Enter* **Antony**, **Octavius**,
          Messala, **Lucilius**, *and the army.*

Octavius
What man is that?

1   *can but make a fire of him*

Can do nothing more than burn his body (rather than be able to celebrate his capture)

2   *entertain them*

Take them into my service

3   **Antony**

Antony's last speech heaps significant praise on the dead Brutus and raises a number of questions that affect how we understand the play. Brutus is now represented as *the noblest Roman of them all*, but is this a judgment with which the audience can concur? It may well be that Brutus does represent all that is noble about Rome and that we should see him as a Stoic hero who acts not out of personal motives but for the common good. Or it may be that Brutus represents the limitations of the Roman Republic, and his flawed nobility only represents the failure of his creed and that of the society he served. Alternatively, we might read the speech in terms of what it tells us about Antony. Some commentators have suggested that these words help to redeem Antony and prepare us for his role in *Antony and Cleopatra* as a flawed but charismatic hero who shows nobility in his loyalty to friends and lovers even when he knows that there is no advantage in such allegiances. Yet perhaps it only reveals his sentimental lack of pragmatism and an inability to think clearly and carefully, which shows what a disastrous leader Antony will prove to be and how easily he can be undermined and defeated by those better suited to rule, like Octavius. However we understand Brutus's epitaph, Antony is also delivering the epitaph for the Roman Republic, and in this sense suggests that Brutus's death may be of greater significance than that of Caesar.

4   *envy of*

Malice toward

5   *in a general honest thought / And common good to all*

With honorable intentions and a concern for the common good

Messala

My master's man.—Strato, where is thy master?

Strato

Free from the bondage you are in, Messala.

The conquerors can but make a fire of him,[1]   55

alone   For Brutus only° overcame himself,

And no man else hath honor by his death.

Lucilius

Like this   So° Brutus should be found.—I thank thee, Brutus,

That thou hast proved Lucilius' saying true.

Octavius

All that served Brutus, I will entertain them.[2]   60

—Fellow, wilt thou bestow thy time with me?

Strato

recommend Aye, if Messala will prefer° me to you.

Octavius

Do so, good Messala.

Messala

How died my master, Strato?

Strato

I held the sword, and he did run on it.

Messala

serve   Octavius, then take him to follow° thee,   65

That did the latest service to my master.

Antony [3]

This was the noblest Roman of them all.

All the conspirators save only he

Did that they did in envy of[4] great Caesar.

alone   He only,° in a general honest thought   70

became   And common good to all,[5] made° one of them.

noble   His life was gentle° and the elements

So mixed in him that Nature might stand up

And say to all the world, "This was a man."

Octavius

According to his virtue let us use him,   75
With all respect and rites of burial.
Within my tent his bones tonight shall lie
treated   Most like a soldier, ordered° honorably.
the armies So call the field° to rest, and let's away
divide up   To part° the glories of this happy day.   *They all exit.*   80

Longer Notes

PAGE 43

1.1.0.1 Flavius, Murellus

Flavius and Murellus are tribunes, government officials representing the people. Here, however, they are scornful of the commoners, who seem to set no value on their own independence (see note to 1.1.36). The triumph of Caesar over Pompey, which the commoners celebrate, marks the beginning of the end of the Roman Republic. The Republic, a balanced state with a constitution that tried to reflect the different elements within its society, was famous—particularly in 16th-century England—as a model form of proto-democratic government.

The period in which the play is set witnessed the accelerating destruction of the Republic, as the elements within Roman society fought each other and eroded the robust checks and balances that had been established to make it work. Rome was partly a victim of its own success as its imperial expansion meant that no one had overall control over the peoples that had been conquered and assimilated into the Republic, even as the army grew in power and threatened the civilian constitution. Julius Caesar, when he crossed the Rubicon, effectively declared war on the Republic, and his victories over his rivals made him dictator.

PAGE 51

1.2.20 *ides of March*

Given Murellus's reference in the previous scene to the feast of Lupercal, which takes place on the 15th of February (1.1.66), we can see how the action in the play works along a double time scheme, with historical events represented dramatically in the tightly constructed first three acts as if they were taking place over two days. The subject of time and the calendar was a topical one in 1599, when Shakespeare wrote *Julius Caesar*. Julius Caesar himself had sorted out problems with the calendar in 46 B.C. by developing the Julian calendar, but had made himself unpopular in the process as many thought that his actions were an arrogant attempt to assert his superiority over nature itself. In any case, by the 1580s the Julian calendar was also inaccurate by about ten days, causing problems for farmers in particular. Pope Gregory made the necessary corrections in 1582, adding the extra days and so restoring the timing of the seasons. Catholic countries accepted the Gregorian calendar, but Protestant countries refused, making European time extremely complex to coordinate, and by 1599 Easter was five weeks apart for Protestants and Catholics. Hence confusions over time in the play may be designed to represent current disputes

in Elizabethan England, which had a major impact on ordinary peoples' lives, tied as they were to the clock and the calendar.

PAGE 115

2.1.295   *Cato's daughter*

Marcus Porcius Cato (95–46 B.C.) was a man famous for his austere moral code and indifference to the lures of the senses. He was an ally of Pompey and was one of the leading opponents of Caesar, who he felt was threatening Rome's long-standing and hard-won liberties. He committed suicide after the defeat of Pompey rather than fall into his bitter enemy's hands. He is one of the moral heroes in Lucan's *Pharsalia* (see note to 1.1.36). Cato was known as a Stoic, holding that man should be indifferent to the fortunes of the world. Triumph and disaster should be treated equally as matters that the wise individual ignores as best as possible. Portia insists upon her strength of mind and character, proving her *constancy* with her *voluntary wound*, and her right to share her *husband's secrets* (2.1.299–302). It is a sign of his flawed character that he cannot establish a companionate

marriage with his deserving wife.
It is a sign either of her limited
understanding of Stoicism or of
its limitations as a creed and a
philosophy that Portia remains so
devoted to her husband that she
does not notice that her passion-
ate arguments undercut the very
ideal of indifference that Stoicism
cultivated.

THE TRAGEDIE OF
IVLIVS CÆSAR.

Actus Primus. Scœna Prima.

Enter Flauius, Murellus, and certaine Commoners ouer the Stage.

Flauius.

HEnce: home you idle Creatures, get you home:
Is this a Holiday? What, know you not
(Being Mechanicall) you ought not walke
Vpon a labouring day, without the signe
Of your Profession? Speake, what Trade art thou?

Car. Why Sir, a Carpenter.

Mur. Where is thy Leather Apron, and thy Rule?
What dost thou with thy best Apparrell on?
You sir, what Trade are you?

Cobl. Truely Sir, in respect of a fine Workman, I am
but as you would say, a Cobler.

Mur. But what Trade art thou? Answer me directly.

Cob. A Trade Sir, that I hope I may vse, with a safe
Conscience, which is indeed Sir, a Mender of bad soules.

Fla. What Trade thou knaue? Thou naughty knaue,
what Trade?

Cobl. Nay I beseech you Sir, be not out with me: yet
if you be out Sir, I can mend you.

Mur. What mean'st thou by that? Mend mee, thou
sawcy Fellow?

Cob. Why sir, Cobble you.

Fla. Thou art a Cobler, art thou?

Cob. Truly sir, all that I liue by, is with the Awle: I
meddle with no Tradesmans matters, nor womens matters; but withall I am indeed Sir, a Surgeon to old shooes:
when they are in great danger, I recouer them. As proper men as euer trod vpon Neats Leather, haue gone vpon my handy-worke.

Fla. But wherefore art not in thy Shop to day?
Why do'st thou leade these men about the streets?

Cob. Truly sir, to weare out their shooes, to get my
selfe into more worke. But indeede sir, we make Holyday to see Cæsar, and to reioyce in his Triumph.

Mur. Wherefore reioyce?
What Conquest brings he home?
What Tributaries follow him to Rome,
To grace in Captiue bonds his Chariot Wheeles?
You Blockes, you stones, you worse then senslesse things:
O you hard hearts, you cruell men of Rome,
Knew you not Pompey many a time and oft?
Haue you climb'd vp to Walles and Battlements,
To Towres and Windowes? Yea, to Chimney tops,
Your Infants in your Armes, and there haue sate
The liue-long day, with patient expectation,

To see great Pompey passe the streets of Rome:
And when you saw his Chariot but appeare,
Haue you not made an Vniuersall shout,
That Tyber trembled vnderneath her bankes
To heare the replication of your sounds,
Made in her Concaue Shores?
And do you now put on your best attyre?
And do you now cull out a Holyday?
And do you now strew Flowers in his way,
That comes in Triumph ouer Pompeyes blood?
Be gone,
Runne to your houses, fall vpon your knees,
Pray to the Gods to intermit the plague
That needs must light on this Ingratitude.

Fla. Go, go, good Countrymen, and for this faule
Assemble all the poore men of your sort;
Draw them to Tyber bankes, and weepe your teares
Into the Channell, till the lowest streame
Do kisse the most exalted Shores of all.

Exeunt all the Commoners.

See where their basest mettle be not mou'd,
They vanish tongue-tyed in their guiltinesse:
Go you downe that way towards the Capitoll,
This way will I: Disrobe the Images,
If you do finde them deckt with Ceremonies.

Mur. May we do so?
You know it is the Feast of Lupercall.

Fla. It is no matter, let no Images
Be hung with Cæsars Trophees: Ile about,
And driue away the Vulgar from the streets;
So do you too, where you perceiue them thicke.
These growing Feathers, pluckt from Cæsars wing,
Will make him flye an ordinary pitch,
Who else would soare aboue the view of men,
And keepe vs all in seruile fearefulnesse. *Exeunt*

Enter Cæsar, Antony for the Course, Calphurnia, Portia, De-
cius, Cicero, Brutus, Cassius, Caska, a Soothsayer: af-
ter them Murellus and Flauius.

Cæs. Calphurnia.

Cask. Peace ho, Cæsar speakes.

Cæs. Calphurnia.

Calp. Heere my Lord.

Cæs. Stand you directly in Antonio's way,
When he doth run his course. *Antonio.*

Ant. Cæsar, my Lord.

Cæs. Forget not in your speed Antonio,
To touch Calphurnia: for our Elders say,

k k   The

A reproduction of the first page of *Julius Caesar* in the First Folio (1623).

Editing *Julius Caesar*
by David Scott Kastan

T he earliest text of *Julius Caesar* is that which was published in the Folio of 1623, though the play was written probably early in 1599. It appears in the Folio as the sixth of the tragedies, printed between *Timon of Athens* and *Macbeth*. The Folio text is apparently based upon scribal transcript of a carefully worked draft of the play. It is in general a clean and orderly text, marred mainly by a few common errors from the printing house: a few obvious spelling errors, some mislineation, and some incorrectly assigned speeches or dropped speech prefixes. Stage directions are quite full and explicit, more so than they would be if this were an authorial draft but not as exact as they would need to be if this had been intended to serve as the prompt copy for performance.

The editorial work of this present edition is conservative, usually a matter of correcting obvious errors, normalizing spelling, capitalization, and punctuation, removing superfluous italics, regularizing the names of characters, and rationalizing entrances and exits. A comparison of the edited text of 1.1.1–1.2.9 with the facsimile page of the Folio (on the opposite page) reveals some of the issues in modernization. The speech prefixes are expanded for clarity, so that *Fla.* is expanded to Flavius and *Mur.* to **Murellus**, just as *Car.* is expanded to **Carpenter** and *Cob.* to **Cobbler**. As spelling in Shakespeare's time

had not yet stabilized, words were spelled in various ways that indi-
cated their proximate pronunciation, and compositors, in any case,
were under no obligation to follow the spelling of their copy. Since
the copy for *Julius Caesar* seems almost certainly to be based on a scribal
transcript, the spelling of the Folio text is at least two removes from
Shakespeare's own hand. Little, then, is to be gained in an edition such
as this by following the spelling of the original printed text. Therefore
"figne" in line 4 unproblematically becomes "sign" in this text, and
"sawcy" (with a "long s") in line 18 becomes "saucy." Old spellings are
consistently modernized, but old *forms* of words (i.e., "dost" in line 8)
are retained. The capitalized first letters of many nouns in the Folio
(e.g., "Proffession" and "Trade" in line 5) are reduced to lowercase, except where modern punctuation would demand them. The italics of
proper names (e.g., "*Pompey*" in line 36) are all removed. Punctuation,
too, is adjusted to reflect modern practice (which is designed to clarify
the logical relations between grammatical units, unlike seventeenth-
century punctuation, which was dominated by rhythmical concerns),
since the punctuation is no more likely than the spelling or capitalization to be Shakespeare's own. Thus, 1.1.34–41 reads in the Folio:

> You Blockes, you stones, you worse then senseless things:
> O you hard hearts, you cruell men of Rome,
> Knew you not *Pompey* many a time and oft?
> Have you climb'd vp to Walles and Battlements,
> To Towres and Windowes? Yea, to Chimney tops,
> Your infants in your Armes, and there haue sate
> The liue-long day, with patient expectation,
> To see great *Pompey* passe the streets of Rome:

Modernized this reads:

> You blocks, you stones, you worse than senseless things,
> O you hard hearts, you cruel men of Rome,

Knew ye not Pompey? Many a time and oft
Have you climbed up to walls and battlements,
To towers and windows, yea, to chimney tops,
Your infants in your arms, and there have sat
The livelong day with patient expectation
To see great Pompey pass the streets of Rome.

No doubt there is some loss in modernization. Clarity and consistency is gained at the expense of some loss of expressive detail, but normalizing spelling, capitalization, and punctuation allows the text to be read with far greater ease than the original, and essentially as it was intended to be understood. Seventeenth-century readers would have been unsurprised to find "v" for "u" in "vp" or "u" for "v" in "liue-long." The intrusive "e" in words like "Walles" (line 37) would not have seemed odd, nor would the "literary" capitalization of the noun. As spelling itself had not normalized, "then" in the first line of the Folio passage above would have been easily understood as "than," as we would spell it today. The colon that ends the passage does not function like a modern colon, defining a particular logical relation between the clauses it separates, but instead functions largely rhythmically, marking a pause slightly less heavy than a period.

For the most part, such modernizing clarifies rather than alters Shakespeare's intentions. If, inevitably in modernization we lose the historical feel of the text Shakespeare's contemporaries read, it is important to note that Shakespeare's contemporaries would not have thought the Folio in any sense archaic or quaint, as these details inevitably make it for a reader today. The text would have seemed to them as modern as this one does to us. Indeed many of the Folio's typographical peculiarities are the result of its effort to make the printed page look up-to-date for potential buyers. Modern readers, however, cannot help but be distracted by the different conventions they encounter on the Folio page. While it is indeed of interest to see how orthography and

typography have changed over time, these changes are not primary
concerns for most readers of this edition. What little, then, is lost in
a careful modernization of the text is more than made up for by the
removal of the artificial obstacle of unfamiliar spelling forms and punctuation habits, which Shakespeare (and his publishers) never could
have intended as interpretive difficulties for his readers.

Textual Notes

The list below records all substantive departures in this edition from
the Folio text of 1623. It does not record modernizations of spelling,
corrections of obvious typographical errors, adjustments of linea-
tion, rationalizations of speech prefixes (SP), or minor repositioning
or rewording of stage directions. The adopted reading in this edition is
given first in boldface and followed by the original, rejected reading of
the Folio, or noted as being absent from the Folio text. Editorial stage
directions (SD) are not collated but are enclosed within brackets in the
text. Latin stage directions are translated into English (e.g., *They all exit*
for *Exeunt omnes*), and the Latin act and scene designation of the Folio are
similarly translated (e.g., Act 1, scene 1 for *Actus primus, scena prima*), with
scene numbers added as they are otherwise absent from the Folio text.

1.1.14 **soles** soules; 1.3.129 **In** Is; 2.1.246 **wafture** wafter; 2.2.46 **are** heare;
2.3.1SP **Artemidorus** [not in F]; 3.1.39 **law** lane; 3.1.113 **states** state; 3.1.115
lies lye; 3.1.210 **strucken** stroken; 3.1.256SP **Antony** [not in F]; 3.1.285 **catching, for** catching from; 3.2.10SD **goes into the pulpit** [at 3.2.0.1 in Folio];
3.2.201SP **All** [not in F]; 3.2.217 **wit** writ; 4.2.34SP **First Soldier** [not in F];
4.2.35SP **Second Soldier** [not in F]; 4.2.36SP **Third Soldier** [not in F]; 4.2.50
Lucius Lucilius; 4.2.52 **Lucilius** Lucius; 4.3.171 **tenor** Tenure; 4.3.253 **will not**
will it not; 5.1.42 **teeth** teethes; 5.2.4 **Octavius'** Octauio's; 5.3.97 **whe'er**
where; 5.3.97 **have not crowned** [some copies of F read: haue crown'd];
5.3.101 **more** mo [some copies of F read: no]; 5.3.104 **Thasos** Tharsus; 5.4.7SP
[not in F]; 5.4.12SP **First Soldier** Sold.; 5.4.15SP **First Soldier** Sold.; 5.4.17
the thee; 5.4.30 **whe'er** where; 5.5.33 **thee too** thee, to; 5.5.40 **life's** liues

Julius Caesar on the Early Stage
by Andrew Hadfield

t is very hard for us to know how Shakespeare's plays were first produced as so little evidence survives before the Restoration, nearly fifty years after Shakespeare's death. In fact, *Julius Caesar* is one of the few plays that can boast a contemporary eyewitness report, that of the Swiss traveler Thomas Platter, who went to see it at the Globe in 1599:

On the 21st of September, after dinner, at about two o'clock, I went with my party across the water; in the straw-thatched house, we saw the tragedy of the first Emperor Julius Caesar, very pleasingly performed, with approximately fifteen characters; at the end of the play they danced together admirably and exceedingly gracefully, according to their custom, two in each group dressed in men's and two women's apparel.

It is not a great deal of information to work on, but Platter's comments do provide us with some tantalizing glimpses of how the theater might have seemed to audiences in the 1590s and why some people went to see plays. Platter makes it clear that he is taken by the spectacle of the theater rather than by the substance of what he has seen performed, commenting more on the dance—a jig, which had formal and complex rules—after the play than the play itself.

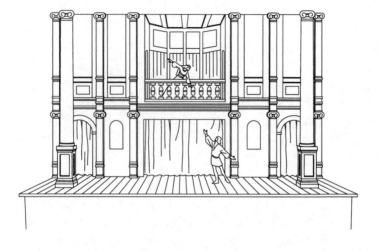

Fig 1. In the large London playhouses, the balcony above the stage could be used for staging, seating, or to house musicians.

Fig 2. English Renaissance drama made minimal use of sets or backdrops. In the absence of a set, the stage pillars could be incorporated into the action, standing in for trees and other architectural elements.

Fig 3. The discovery space, located in the middle of the backstage wall, could be used as a third entrance as well as a location for scenes requiring special staging, such as in a tomb or bedchamber.

Fig 4. A trapdoor led to the area below the stage, known as "Hell" (as contrasted with the painted ceiling, known as "Heaven" or the "heavens"). Ghosts or other supernatural figures could descend through the trap, and it could also serve as a grave.

He notes that about fifteen actors were used, which is what we have learned elsewhere was the usual cast size for a London play (touring productions in the provinces invariably used fewer actors). It is also worth observing that he comments on the dancers being dressed as men and women. Women did not appear on the professional London stage until after the Restoration (1660); all acting parts were taken by male actors, with women's roles usually played by boys. This cross-dressing practice was unusual, as many European theaters did employ actors of both sexes, hence the Swiss Platter's feeling that this was worthy of note.

The London commercial theater really only dates from the late 1570s, and had started to form a central part of London life in the decade and a half before Platter's visit. New theaters were being built, and by 1600 there were six in London, including the Swan, the Red Bull, the Rose, and the Globe, all of which had the capacity for an audience of between about five hundred and perhaps three thousand. As London was a city of about 200,000 people, clearly a large percentage of its adult population were regular theatergoers, and great pressure was put on companies to produce plays at a rapid rate so that they could keep up with audience demand. Companies rehearsed one play in the morning and performed another in the afternoon, making sure that they had a varied repertoire and a constant stock of new drama.

It is easy to see why Platter would have been taken to the Globe. It was a new theater and an obvious landmark in the city, visible from most vantage points adjacent to the Thames and clearly designed to lure audiences. The Globe was a large, impressive building with a capacity of about fifteen hundred spectators. It was, like the Rose and other theaters, a substantial circular building with a thatched roof covering the seated areas inside, leaving the central area of the building exposed to the weather. The stage was at one end, with seating arranged around the rest of the building. The central area constituted a space for standing customers who would simply have to brave the elements if it rained. It is unthinkable that Platter and his company would not have been seated.

The theater was an innovative and exciting new development in London that played an unstable role in the life of the city, making its critics anxious about its impact. There are many contemporary complaints about the behavior of audiences and the impact of the entertainments that they enjoyed. Some puritanical critics felt that the theaters, which were situated outside the city walls and so escaped the restrictions and regulations approved by London's governing elite, encouraged vice. Given that the theaters were in areas next to brothels and taverns, and were sometimes owned by less than respectable businessmen, they undoubtedly had a point. Obviously such commentators disapproved of plays, especially the elements of fantasy and social critique that many contained, as well as the opportunities that actors had to subvert the norms of everyday life by dressing up as women, aristocrats, and kings. But we need to be careful of assuming that drama had the power to inspire and offend as much as we might want it to have done.

We should also bear in mind that early modern theater audiences probably did not behave quite as we do now when we go to the theater. The authorities were frequently worried about the large crowds, often made up of rowdy, drunken young men, who gathered to watch the plays and other entertainments that took place in theaters and similar public arenas, such as dancing and bearbaiting. We should not assume that everyone who went to the theater was interested in sophisticated, thought-provoking drama. But when they did go, what did they want to see and how did they respond to what they saw? Experiments at the restored Globe recently built in London suggest that audiences were often noisy and irreverent, keen to get involved in the action of the play they saw, taking sides, applauding good characters and booing and hissing bad ones. There are many complaints about the behavior of audiences before the theaters were

ordered closed in 1642 when the forces hostile to popular entertain-
ment were for a brief period triumphant.

Such evidence suggests ways in which we might think about
the early staging of *Julius Caesar*. What I say has to be speculative but
is in line with the little that we know about the London theater and
its audience in 1599. Given that *Julius Caesar* was probably the first play
staged at the Globe, it is fair to assume that it must have been chosen because of its popular appeal. Everybody knew the story; it was
dramatic and would hold the interest of those present, and it raised a
whole series of contemporary political concerns.

It is easy to imagine an audience responding enthusiastically
to Brutus's claims at the start of the play and imagining that killing
Caesar was justified, but then changing tack and supporting Antony
when he skillfully undermines the moral authority of the conspirators in his speech over the body of Caesar. The players may well have
appealed directly to different parts of the theater, and different sec-
tions might have responded in different ways, the audience dividing
up into factions. Perhaps the last two acts were observed in a relatively
muted manner, the audience having exhausted itself, rather like the
Roman factions.

Julius Caesar undoubtedly seemed an ideal work to stage
in a big, new theater. It required a relatively large cast that could be
exploited to give a sense of the chaos induced by a violent and shocking event, especially if we bear in mind the restricted space available in
the earlier theaters. The first staging of *Julius Caesar* probably saw the
play produced as a political drama, centering the early action on the
nervous and paranoid plotting of the conspirators; the middle sec-
tions on the assassination and its aftermath; and the final section on
the protracted civil war that eventually led to the destruction of the
republicans and their ideals. The quarrel between Brutus and Cassius
has not always held the attention of modern audiences, but it was
one of the most popular sequences in Shakespeare's canon in the

eighteenth century, and we should assume that early modern audiences had a similarly enthusiastic reaction to the tragic denouement of Brutus and Cassius's noble friendship.

The acting would have had to be forceful and vigorous, since the speeches, especially those made over Caesar's corpse, are designed to persuade a hostile audience that the action taken is right, then wrong. Shakespeare, as in so many of his plays, draws the audience into the world of the play. The audience, in effect, stands for the nervous Roman citizens and is forced to interpret what it sees in the light of the play on the stage as well as what individual spectators might have thought about contemporary events. We should probably imagine the speakers playing directly to the audience, drawing them into the arguments that they were advocating, involving them in the illusion of the play and so making it relevant to their own lives. Some spectators would undoubtedly have felt that Caesar, whatever his flaws, should have been left to rule as he saw fit; others, that the republican assassins had a point even if what they began could not be controlled. It is hard to imagine that anyone leaving the theater felt comfortable about what they had witnessed. The play begins showing powerful and influential citizens clustered in groups behaving secretively in ways that go against the spirit of the ideals they serve; it ends with an exhausted and miserable triumph which we know is only one phase in a brutal civil war. How far an audience read this as Shakespeare's vision of late Elizabethan England is a question worth asking, even if a definite answer is unlikely to emerge. Much recent criticism has stressed that early modern drama developed out of a culture of argument, specifically an educated system that was designed to develop rhetorical and logical skills by arguing both sides of an issue. *Julius Caesar* clearly fits such a pattern.

Shakespeare's play promised to be topical and risqué, but also dramatic and full of human interest with characters who were larger than life. The audience could be manipulated one way and another as the drama developed. As most critics have noted, *Julius*

Caesar does not take sides in any easy way. Both Caesar and Brutus are flawed characters, as are Cassius and Antony. But there is also great nobility in the decaying ideals of the Republic and its faith in a just, public culture. There is also much to admire in the friendship of both Brutus and Cassius, and Caesar and Antony, as well as the loyal commitments of Portia and Calphurnia. Caesar is not an obvious tyrant and Brutus is not an evil assassin. In short, the play alludes to a whole series of issues vitally relevant to a nervous and threatened country such as England, subsumed with fear of the future, surrounded by enemies, and terrified of the descent into a bloody civil war. Equally importantly, it does not provide easy answers to burning topical questions while making sure that their urgency (and perhaps unanswerability) is established by the play's carefully patterned and charged language.

Early modern theaters did make effective use of props when staging plays. However, it would appear that the major emphasis was placed on the verbal quality of the plays, the arguments they staged, and the speeches characters made to persuade other characters and the audience that they were right, which would explain why *Julius Caesar* was such a popular play. In fact, the play requires very little in the way of expensive or elaborate props to set the scene. The words establish where we are and what is important. The connections that audiences made with contemporary events were undoubtedly enhanced by this relaxed attitude to history, links that *Julius Caesar* clearly encourages its audience to consider.

There is less evidence about sets, early modern acting styles, and costumes than we would like to have. An interesting reference appears in Philip Henslowe's diary, the records kept by the owner of the Rose Theatre in the 1590s. Henslowe kept details of his professional dealings and the running of his company. In 1598 he made an inventory of the props acquired for plays which includes an entry for "ij marchepanes [a type of ornamental almond cake] and the sittie of Rome." What might this "sittie [city] of Rome" have been? It was probably a curtain or a tapestry of some form that would have been hung at the back of the stage as a backdrop to represent the city. There are references elsewhere to "hangings" depicting tragic scenes behind the actors so it was evidently a contemporary stage practice. It is likely that a similar—perhaps even the same—backdrop was used in *Julius Caesar*, but the stage would have been largely bare, with a few chairs or tables moved on and off as they were required.

The only significant illustration of the staging of a Shakespeare play made during the author's lifetime is Henry Peacham's drawing of *Titus Andronicus*. As this is another Roman play it might help to provide some clues that might help us interpret how *Julius Caesar* was first staged. Peacham's drawing, assuming that it is accurate, shows seven figures on stage. Titus Andronicus himself is dressed in a Roman toga. He confronts Tamora, the Queen of the Goths, who appears to wear a costume of a contemporary queen rather than an authentically reconstructed historical costume. The other figures also seem to be wearing Elizabethan dress, not Roman or Goth costume.

Peacham's memory may be faulty. Nevertheless, the way he represents the play suggests that historically accurate costume was not necessarily primary among the concerns of Elizabethan playwrights or the expectations of their audiences. The text of *Julius Caesar* indicates that Caesar was not dressed in period costume. When Casca describes Caesar's dramatic refusal of the crown it is clear that the actor playing Caesar was dressed as an Elizabethan gentleman: "when he perceived the common herd was glad he refused the crown, he plucked me ope his doublet and offered them his throat to cut." (1.2.265–268). Perhaps none of the actors in the play wore authentic costume and Rome was represented simply by a backdrop. Perhaps, as in the Peacham illustration, there was an eclectic mixture of costumes worn. In any case, with no extensive effort to make Julius Caesar's Rome physically present, Shakespeare's language has brought it vividly and enduringly to life.

Significant Performances
by Andrew Hadfield

June 1599   *Julius Caesar* is the first play performed at the Globe, the new home of Shakespeare's acting company. Swiss traveler Thomas Platter provides an eyewitness account of the production. He says little about the play but does record that he enjoyed the performance and that he thought it was a notable event (for further discussion, see "*Julius Caesar* on the Early Stage," page 291).

1611–1612   Whitehall (first recorded court performance)

January 31, 1636   St. James's Palace

1719   John Dryden and William Davenant stage their rewritten version of the play in London. After the Restoration, ancient Rome became fashionable as both an aesthetic ideal and an interesting political subject, as many wondered whether the political in-fighting and intrigues that characterized Roman government might serve as a useful model for understanding life at the English court. Roman social behavior was often imitated by the English aristocracy, who wanted to model their lives on Roman ideals of noble bearing in public, sophisticated detachment to the vicissitudes of public life, and cultural sophistication. Dryden and Davenant rewrote much of the play in order to make the characters seem nobler, as they believed

Shakespeare had originally intended (the vulgar age Shakespeare lived in having prevented him from carrying out his aims properly). Brutus now had a new speech to preface his suicide, one fitting a dignified hero and patriot who made the decision to take his own life rather than suffer the shame of capture, trial, and execution.

1812–1819   John Philip Kemble stages the play at the Theatre Royal, Covent Garden, in a production that continues to run until his retirement. Kemble made the play an expression of noble ideals, paying close attention to all forms of detail. Beautiful sets were constructed (Kemble was a friend of Sir Joshua Reynolds, the preeminent English artist of the day), which complemented the actors' careful and studious elocution. The production met with great public success, ensuring its long run.

1838–1839   Covent Garden; 1843, Drury Lane. In many ways the actor-manager W. C. Macready, who played Cassius and Brutus in different productions, carried on where Kemble had left off, preserving the noble and aristocratic style of Kemble's production. Macready made use of the large cast to place an even greater emphasis on the crowd scenes, representing Rome as a vibrant and populous city. The assassination scene became a notable event—setting the scene for later nineteenth-century productions—which demonstrated how shock waves could ripple through society, the large cast showing how chaos could be generated by one carefully planned event. Macready, who dominated the performances, became a significant celebrity.

1846–1862   Samuel Phelps stages the play at Sadler's Wells in London. Phelps's productions were more spare and restricted than those of Macready and Kemble, making use of more basic sets. Phelps, who played a dignified Brutus, was less dominating than Macready but often had to work with a cast of limited actors.

1870s and 1880s Georg II, ruler of the German duchy of Saxe-Meiningen, tours Europe with his production of *Julius Caesar*, which is performed in German at Drury Lane in May 1881. Antony assumed a central role in these surprisingly successful productions. As in Macready's productions, the assassination scenes were played to great effect, successfully representing the panic and chaos of the drama for the enraptured audience. The emphasis on the crowd scenes and the political significance of the play pointed toward later twentieth-century developments.

1871 Edwin Booth stages the play in New York. American productions tended to be much more sympathetic to Brutus, who was seen as a noble patriot struggling against ancient tyranny. Booth's production was grand, opulent, and made use of an elaborate classical set complete with towering columns and statues. Booth's Brutus was a committed idealist of considerable passion, while also being fallible and human in his failure to live up to the standards he set himself. Booth later played Cassius with considerable success.

1898 Herbert Beerbohm Tree stages the play at Her Majesty's Theatre, London. Perhaps the most spectacular version of the play ever staged, with an immense cast, a crowded and colorful stage, and spectacular scenes. Antony also dominated the play—the text was cut to showcase his character—and was represented in much more sympathetic terms than the conspirators. As in many later productions, the funeral oration assumed a central importance.

1890–1930 Frank Benson stages the play at the Shakespeare Memorial Theatre in Stratford-upon-Avon. Benson used a drastically cut text and staged his productions on a much smaller and more human scale than Beerbohm Tree had, using little scenery on the small stage in the theater. Caesar was represented as powerful but past his peak and fading fast.

1919–1934   William Bridges-Adams stages the play at the Shakespeare Memorial Theatre. An important series of productions that played the text largely uncut, perhaps for the first time in 250 years. The reduced sets facilitated a fast and athletic production, which concentrated on the words rather than the scenery.

1937   Orson Welles directs and plays Brutus in a production subtitled "Death of a Dictator" at the Mercury Theater in New York. Welles's updated production—one of the first to make clear parallels between the play and contemporary events, which became a recurring feature of twentieth-century productions—struck a chord with the American public and ran for 157 performances. The set used claustrophobic, blood-red walls and made an explicit link between Caesar's triumphs and the rise of Fascism in 1930s Europe. The text was heavily cut in order to accommodate Welles's political message. Brutus was cast as a feeble liberal eventually spurred into action. The play successfully staged the terrible effects of mob violence, particularly with its shocking representation of the murder of Cinna, a scene that had not always been performed in earlier productions but was here depicted as a brutal lynching. Other productions in the late 1930s made the same links as Welles, but often with less success.

1950   John Barton stages an original pronunciation production of the play with the Marlowe Society of Cambridge University. The aim of this experimental student production was to reproduce what had happened at the Globe in 1599, anticipating more recent attempts to produce the same effect, such as the original pronunciation performance of *Romeo and Juliet* at the new Globe in 2004. Many of Barton's audience members found the production incomprehensible due to the unfamiliar nature of the language and the sometimes rather amateurish efforts of the actors to pronounce the text they had been given.

1953   Joseph L. Mankiewicz directs a Hollywood film version of the play, which is notable for its impressive large crown scenes. John Gielgud was cast as an intense, nervous Cassius and James Mason as a naïve but thoughtful Brutus who did not take any decision lightly. Against them Marlon Brando played a powerful, brooding, and physical Antony, with Lewis Calhern as a weak Caesar.

1968   John Barton stages the play with the Royal Shakespeare Company (RSC). This was another production that made the link between the dictatorial Caesar, played by Brewster Mason, and authoritarian government, which had critics comparing Caesar to General de Gaulle.

1972   Trevor Nunn staged this revival of the play at the RSC. Many commentators have singled this production out as the best in living memory. The set had a massive statue of Caesar, resembling Mussolini, dominating the actors who were dwarfed by his presence. This design element was widely praised, although some observers argued that there was an absence of subtlety in the approach. Brutus, played by John Wood, was again cast as a smug liberal out of his depth in murky power politics. The role of Octavius assumed greater importance than he had previously, and was integrated into the main plot rather than left as an adjunct to the main action.

1972   Jonathan Miller directed this experimental production with the Oxford and Cambridge Company. Miller staged the play in a terrifying dream world, ruled by the supernatural and superstition. The actors spoke in stilted slow motion to emphasize what the director saw as the strange and surreal world of the play. The approach confused many audience members and critics were not wholly convinced that this was a successful experiment.

1977   John Schlesinger directs the play at the National Theatre of London. This production represented Caesar, played by John Gielgud, as a natural leader with great personal authority. Even his Ghost seemed to have more control over events than the other characters on stage, emphasizing Caesar's charismatic authority and the dependence of the other characters on the example of the man whose power they had come to resent so bitterly.

1978   BBC/Time Life produces a television version of the play. The small screen production enabled the human drama of the play to be given greater emphasis than in film versions, and also serves as a useful corrective to the many politically inspired productions of the later twentieth century. Brutus, played by Richard Pasco, was disturbed, driven, and vulnerable; Charles Gay's Caesar was both imperious and jovial, confidently inhabiting a male-dominated world.

1987   Terry Hands staging for the RSC was notable for being a relatively minimalist production, which avoided the large crowd scenes of recent productions.

1993   David Thacker directs the play at The Other Place, one of the RSC's smaller performance venues in Stratford-upon-Avon. This production cast Caesar as a woman, alluding to the then British prime minister, Margaret Thatcher.

2005 Daniel Sullivan's Broadway production cast Denzel Washington as Brutus, generating significant publicity but rather mixed reviews. The play was set in contemporary America, a maneuver that, perhaps inevitably, created a series of anachronisms and strange effects. Many critics complained that the ingenuity demanded to make the parallels work between life in contemporary USA and classical Rome detracted from the action. Washington was felt to be rather limited by many reviewers, who praised the rest of the cast.

Inspired by *Julius Caesar*

Although Shakespeare was not the first to chronicle the life of Julius Caesar—his version of events draws heavily on the work of ancient Greek historian Plutarch—it is his play that has captured the imagination of readers and audiences over the centuries, becoming perhaps the most famous work of art about the legendary Roman leader. Dialogue such as the Soothsayer's infamous warning "Beware the ides of March," Caesar's final "*Et tu, Brutè?*" and Antony's funeral lament "Friends, Romans, countrymen, lend me your ears" have filtered into our common cultural vocabulary, recognizable even to those who have never read or seen *Julius Caesar*. For many readers, the only knowledge they have of the historical figure comes from Shakespeare's play, which focuses its attention on the final, fraught days of the dictator's life.

Since 1599, when *Julius Caesar* was first performed at the Globe Theatre in London, artworks that attempt to portray Caesar's life invariably invite comparisons to Shakespeare's play, and many such works of drama, film, and literature explicitly respond to Shakespeare's version of events. Perhaps the most famous theatrical event inspired by *Julius Caesar*, however, was not a work of art at all but a shocking act of political retaliation. The April 14, 1865, assassination of Abraham Lincoln at the Ford Theater by John Wilkes Booth was eerily haunted by Shakespeare's play. Born into a family of actors—and having recently played Antony in a Booth family production of *Julius Caesar*—Booth saw Lincoln as a tyrannous Caesar and himself as a liberating Brutus who would free the oppressed Confederates. (Booth's own father was named after Lucius Junius Brutus, ancestor of Shakespeare's Brutus.) A diary entry from the fateful day is marked "Friday the Ides," a reference to the date of Caesar's murder. In another entry written just before his capture, Booth laments, "I am here in despair. And why; For doing what Brutus was honored for . . . And yet I for striking down a greater tyrant than they ever knew am looked upon as a common cutthroat." Booth's self-pitying reference to Brutus points to his delirious fantasy of liberating America from Lincoln, just as Caesar's murderers liberated Rome from Caesar.

Happily, most works inspired by *Julius Caesar* remain confined to the stage, the screen, or the page. In the mid-1800s, an anonymous British playwright updated Shakespeare's characters in a melodramatic variety show entitled *Julius Caesar, Travestie*. The performance drew on both the popularity of burlesque theater and the trend of using Shakespeare's plays to parody contemporary political figures. In this vein, Caesar is portrayed more as a slimy politician than a strong dictator. *Julius Caesar, Travestie* is interlaced with popular songs and jokes, many of which are aimed at foreigners and current events.

In 1898, George Bernard Shaw wrote *Caesar and Cleopatra*, perhaps the most famous dramatic version of Caesar's life after Shakespeare's own. Shaw's play precedes the events of both *Julius Caesar* and Shakespeare's *Antony and Cleopatra*, depicting the period in which a much younger Caesar and Cleopatra were lovers. In *Caesar and Cleopatra*, Shaw places Caesar at the very center of his play, rather than leaving him on the fringes of the main action as Shakespeare does. Shaw's version also differs from Shakespeare's in its diligent attention to historical detail. _Julius Caesar_ famously contains many anachronisms, such as clocks, sleeves, and books, none of which existed during Caesar's lifetime. Shaw, on the other hand, took pains to consult with Egyptologists and research the scientific technology available to Romans and in the epilogue to _Caesar and Cleopatra_ he explicitly points out the moments where his play consciously deviates from historical truth.

In 1907, French filmmaker Georges Méliès shot a silent five-minute film called _Le Rêve de Shakespeare_, which translates to "A Dream of Shakespeare" but is frequently referred to as "Shakespeare Writing _Julius Caesar_." In the fantastical short, Méliès, an early and innovative film pioneer, plays Shakespeare, who is inspired to write _Julius Caesar_ after he daydreams a vision of Caesar's murder. _Le Rêve de Shakespeare_ emphasizes the visual element of imagination, destined to flourish through the new medium of film, versus the literary and linguistic element usually associated with Shakespeare. In the same year, Méliès also filmed a brief adaptation of _Hamlet_.

In 1948, Thornton Wilder resurrected _Julius Caesar_ in his acclaimed experimental novel _The Ides of March_. The book—the title of which refers to the date of Caesar's assassination—is an epistolary novel, which means that it takes the form of a series of letters exchanged between Caesar, Cleopatra, Antony, and others. In the introduction to his novel, Wilder notes that source material about Caesar's life is marked by curious gaps and incongruities. Wilder attempts to fill in some of the blanks left in the historical record, but his recreation of events is not meant to be a slavishly accurate reconstruction. Rather, he called his fictional documents and correspondence a "fantasia" set in the final days of the Roman Empire. Though epistolary novels can often seem artificial and static, the form allows Wilder to portray a much more human Julius Caesar than Shakespeare's regal sovereign. While Shakespeare avoids revealing any of Caesar's inner thoughts, Wilder's fictitious letters function like dramatic soliloquies, revealing the dictator's personality, private thoughts, and emotions.

Godfrey Grayson's 1959 British film *An Honourable Murder* sets Shakespeare's *Julius Caesar* in the world of corporate power and greed. In the film, the ruthless board of directors at a large company schemes to overthrow their struggling chairman, Julian Caesar. Caesar dies of a heart attack after being voted off the board and Mark Anthony avenges his death with a moving speech to the investors followed by the firing of the corrupt directors, including R. Cassius and Brutus Smith.

Theodore White's 1968 play *Caesar at the Rubicon* portrays Julius Caesar as a robust young general rather than the dignified old emperor of Shakespeare's version. *Caesar at the Rubicon* focuses on the moment in which the impetuous Caesar decides to cross the waters of the Rubicon and overtake the Roman Republic, declaring himself dictator. White returns to this seminal moment in Caesar's history so that he can trace how Caesar became emperor, rather than showing the emperor in his decline, as Shakespeare does. White's play is keenly aware of Caesar's legacy, both in history and in fiction. In his prologue, White ruminates on Caesars past. "Shakespeare, drawing him from Plutarch, made him the moody tyrant, creature of fate. . . . Shaw made him the witty, detached adventurer, toying with life and empire as a game . . . In our time, Thornton Wilder has made him the urbane and cynical phrase-maker, world-weary, soul-tired." White, however, claims that the real Caesar was a man ahead of his time, one who would have been much more familiar to a modern audience than understood by his own contemporaries.

John Bowen's *Heil Caesar!* was originally commissioned by the BBC in 1973 as part of their series of drama programs aimed at students. The adaptation was presented as three half-hour segments, directed by Ronald Smedley, but was so successful with audiences and critics that the BBC transferred it to primetime and ran the three episodes together. After the BBC success, *Heil Caesar!* was modified for the stage. Bowen's adaptation is set in an unnamed modern country where Caesar rules as president of a multiparty coalition. This witty political drama presents a satirical view of the often-blurred line between democracy and dictatorship, especially considering the inordinate amount of power held by the privileged classes. *Heil Caesar!* also emphasizes the importance of images and the influence of the media, as the forum speeches are transformed into television appearances.

Julius Caesar figures prominently in the 1999 comedy *Free Enterprise*. Robert and Mark are two would-be filmmakers quickly approaching thirty who show no signs of abandoning the sci-fi and pop culture obsessions of their youth. Frustrated by their lack of professional (and romantic) success, they're thrilled to run into their hero, *Star Trek*'s William Shatner, in a bookstore. Shatner, playing a satirically egomaniacal version of himself, confesses to Robert and Mark that his dearest fantasy is to turn *Julius Caesar* into a rap musical called "No Tears for Caesar," in which he'll play all the parts except for Calpurnia. (That role he'll save for Sharon Stone or Heather Locklear.) As Robert and Mark start to move past their stunted adolescences, Shatner, in a parallel subplot, continues to develop his dream project. At the end of the movie, Shatner triumphantly performs a rap version of Mark Antony's famous funeral elegy, complete with badly synced background music.

The Malaysian theater director Nam Rom uses *Julius Caesar* as a starting point for his 2003 film *Gedebe*, based on his play of the same name. *Gedebe* ("gangster" or "bully") focuses on the underground punk scene in Kuala Lumpur, where Caesar is depicted as a skinhead and Brutus as an undercover cop. With the tag line "Siapa bunuh Caesar?" or "Who killed Caesar?" the film chronicles the days leading up to Caesar's murder. *Gedebe*, which reflects unease over recent political events in Malaysia, is filmed in the Kelantanese dialect but maintains the names of Shakespeare's characters.

For Further Reading
by Andrew Hadfield

Bushnell, Rebecca. "*Julius Caesar.*" In *A Companion to Shakespeare's Works: Vol. 1, The Tragedies.* Ed. Richard Dutton and Jean E. Howard. Oxford: Blackwell, 2003. 339–356. Excellent on the politics and the rhetoric of the play.

Gurr, Andrew. *Playgoing in Shakespeare's London.* 2nd ed. Cambridge: Cambridge University Press, 2000. The best guide to the London stage of Shakespeare's time.

Hadfield, Andrew. *Shakespeare and Republicanism.* Cambridge: Cambridge University Press, 2005. Chapter 5 examines the play in terms of its retelling of the familiar story of the death of the Roman Republic and how this might have been read in 1590s England.

Hamer, Mary. *Julius Caesar.* Writers and their Work. Plymouth: Northcote House, 1998. Quirky but often insightful. Very good on women in the play.

Kahn, Coppélia. *Roman Shakespeare: Warriors, Wounds, and Women.* London: Routledge, 1997. Chapter 4 presents a brilliant reading of the play in terms of ideals of masculinity and femininity.

Le Glay, Marcel, Jean-Louis Voisin, Yann Le Bohec, and David Cherry. *A History of Rome*. Trans. Antonia Nevill. 2nd ed. Oxford: Blackwell, 2001. A comprehensive and detailed history of the city and its role in establishing European civilization.

Liebler, Naomi Conn. *Shakespeare's Festive Tragedy: The Ritual Foundations of Genre*. London: Routledge, 1995. A bold and ambitious study of the anthropological roots of tragedy. Chapter 3 examines the play in terms of ancient sacrificial rituals.

McDonald, Russ. *Shakespeare and the Arts of Language*. Oxford Shakespeare Topics. Oxford: Oxford University Press, 2001. Patiently and clearly explains how to read Shakespeare's verse and prose.

Miles, Geoffrey. *Shakespeare and the Constant Romans*. Oxford: Clarendon Press, 1996. A useful account of Stoicism and manliness in the play.

Miola, Robert. *Shakespeare's Rome*. Cambridge: Cambridge University Press, 1983. Scholarly and lucid overview of the Roman plays.

———"*Julius Caesar* and the Tyrannicide Debate." *Renaissance Quarterly* 38 (1985): 271–289 Explains how the story of Julius Caesar's assassination was represented and read in the sixteenth century as a means of placing the play in context.

Roe, John. *Shakespeare and Machiavelli: Studies in Renaissance Literature*. Cambridge: Brewer, 2002. Chapter 5 presents a sensible and clear reading of the political issues of the play. Good also on its rhetoric.

Shapiro, James. *1599: A Year in the Life of William Shakespeare*. London: Faber, 2005. Chapter 8 provides a superb reading of the play in terms of

Shakespeare's development as a writer and the historical influences that determined its form and substance.

Wiggins, Martin. *Shakespeare and the Drama of his Time*. Oxford Shakespeare Topics. Oxford: Oxford University Press, 2000. Excellent introduction to the varieties of early modern English drama.

Wilson, Richard, ed. *Julius Caesar: Contemporary Critical Essays*. New Casebooks. Basingstoke: Palgrave, 2002. A collection of recent essays on the play that includes Wilson's important work on the representation of holiday in the play, René Girard's essay on violence and sacrifice, Wayne Rebhorn's essay on the crisis of aristocratic values in the play, and many others.